Method to the Madness

Method to the Madness

A Common Core Guide to Creating Critical Thinkers Through the Study of Literature

B.H. James and Elizabeth James

ROWMAN & LITTLEFIELD
Lanham • Boulder • New York • London

Published by Rowman & Littlefield
A wholly owned subsidiary of The Rowman & Littlefield Publishing Group, Inc.
4501 Forbes Boulevard, Suite 200, Lanham, Maryland 20706
www.rowman.com

Unit A, Whitacre Mews, 26-34 Stannary Street, London SE11 4AB

British Library Cataloguing in Publication Information Available

Library of Congress Cataloging-in-Publication Data

Names: James, B. H., 1978- author. | James, Elizabeth, 1984- author.
Title: Method to the madness : a common core guide to creating critical thinkers through the study of literature / B.H. James and Elizabeth James.
Description: Lanham : Rowman & Littlefield, 2016. | Includes bibliographical references and index.
Identifiers: LCCN 2015044205 (print) | LCCN 2016006748 (ebook) | ISBN 9781475825374 (cloth : alk. paper) | ISBN 9781475825381 (pbk. : alk. paper) | ISBN 9781475825398 (Electronic)
Subjects: LCSH: Literature—Study and teaching (Secondary)—United States. | American literature—Study and teaching (Secondary)—United States. | English literature—Study and teaching (Secondary)—United States. | English language—Composition and exercises—Study and teaching (Secondary)—United States. | Critical thinking—Study and teaching (Secondary)—United States.
Classification: LCC PN59 .J36 2016 (print) | LCC PN59 (ebook) | DDC 807.1/273—dc23
LC record available at http://lccn.loc.gov/2015044205

∞™ The paper used in this publication meets the minimum requirements of American National Standard for Information Sciences—Permanence of Paper for Printed Library Materials, ANSI/NISO Z39.48-1992.

Printed in the United States of America

Contents

Preface vii

Acknowledgments xi

Introduction xiii

1 Writing for Critical Thinking and Logical Cohesiveness (Or, How to Survive the Shift to Common Core) 1

2 Begin with Close Reading 14

3 *The Great Gatsby*: Applying the Skills of Close Reading 29

4 *The Taming of the Shrew*: An Introduction to Shakespeare 47

5 Teaching *Hamlet:* Or, How to Approach the Most Important Piece of Literature Ever Written 68

6 Teaching Fiction Writing: The Importance of Allowing Students to Create, Revise, and Publish 90

7 *Slaughterhouse 5* and *The Things They Carried*: Appreciating Postmodern Approaches to Fiction 115

8 Toni Morrison's *Beloved:* Recognizing and Evaluating Theme and Purpose in a Complex Text 140

9 *The Adventures of Huckleberry Finn* and Abraham Lincoln: Designing a Cross-Curricular Unit of Study 156

Index 177

About the Authors 183

Preface

Six years ago, we were each hired to teach a summer school creative writing course in our district. Our classrooms were across the hall from each other. There was no curriculum provided. No pacing guides. No mandated test. The course was designed to be credit recovery, full of kids who had failed an English class the previous year. By working collaboratively that summer, we created a course that was both rigorous and a lot of fun—for the kids and the grown-ups alike.

The students in our classes read great literature—both classic and contemporary—and analyzed the craft of that literature. And they wrote. A lot. And they shared their work and scrutinized their work and revised their work. We didn't keep track then, but the following spring, when we duplicated the same units in our tenth-grade classes, we did keep track, and those students (roughly one hundred of them) collectively generated approximately ten thousand pages of original and revised fiction over the course of one quarter.

There was a third creative writing teacher that year in summer school. Her kids were, according to her, too noisy, not smart enough, just there to hang out, and quickly driving her crazy. What was she doing in class? Diamond poems, acrostic poems, poetry worksheets—the sorts of things you might expect to see at a second-grade back-to-school night. That was when it began to become clear—what was the difference? Why were two of the classes that summer working—and working hard—and one wasn't?

We had no previous rapport with the students—summer school wasn't at our site that year—so these kids had never been in our rooms before. All three classes were populated by students who had failed English classes in the past. All three were full of students who were not necessarily fast-tracked for success. The difference, really, was strikingly simple.

We were teaching them things that were interesting—to us, as readers. And through our enthusiasm and desire to discuss—deeply, analytically—what we found interesting with our students, they became interested, as well.

Why, as educators—as people who presumably love learning—do we so often abandon what made us "nerd out" as students ourselves, and instead prescribe to our students boring and/or substandard reading—most likely prescribed to us by a school board or a publisher—to kids who are struggling with writing and reading? Taking an underachieving urban school, similar to the one we taught in at this time, you can probably count on a few things in that school's textbook room:

1. Big, thick, heavy textbooks that include everything the student will read (or will be assigned to read but won't read) that year. First of all, who wants to curl up with a book that weighs about the same as a sandbag? Second, it has been our observation that such books include second-rate (and safer, and shorter) works by really great authors. Finally, an anecdote: several years back, when districts spent a whole lot of money on textbook adoptions, and teachers were subsequently expected to be spending every minute teaching those textbooks, the ninth-grade English text included Act II of *Romeo and Juliet*. Just Act II. The notion then being that ninth-grade teachers would initiate their often-below-grade-level students to the rich and varied world of Shakespeare by teaching *Romeo and Juliet*, Act II. Just Act II.
2. A collection of short (and often short on craft) novels about a young kid from the streets who wants to be a basketball player, or something similarly cliché, the notion here being that the only way to get struggling readers who don't want to read to read is to give them something they *can relate to*. Like *the streets*. Or *basketball*. If this seems in any way demeaning, we agree with you, and don't believe for a second that the students aren't aware of it. You know what's even more relevant to their lives than *the streets* or *basketball*? Every play Shakespeare wrote, and it's our job to show them how.
3. Stack after stack of quality novels and plays shoved in a corner, gathering dust, because "these kids can't handle books like that."

What we have found was that when we spent time talking about and thinking about literature that personally affected us, we had a much stronger motivation to teach the skills associated with that literature, and teach them well. In contrast, it can be difficult to find the motivation to design an engaging lesson around reading an instructional manual.

Great literature—along with the skills required to read and appreciate it—is interesting to us, English Lit nerds, and through our enthusiasm, it therefore became interesting to our student population.

The following year, we were assigned to team teach at the tenth-grade level. We took the opportunity to overhaul the reading list. Our criterion was books that students should read before getting to college—the books smart people will be talking about. That year, the list consisted of *The Sun Also Rises*, *The Things They Carried*, *Slaughterhouse Five*, *1984*, *The Great Gatsby*, *Death of a Salesman*, and *Macbeth.*

We took that year to test our hypothesis: could you take 180 students of various ability and various backgrounds and find success by mirroring the type of work you would see in a college-level English class. We did our homework—a lot of homework, it turns out, which we used as an opportunity to model for the students. We would bring in our notes and a stack of literary criticism we'd pored through, and would show them that to prepare these lessons, we had had to study up. They appreciated that.

We used itunes U lectures from Yale and Berkeley and Harvard to demonstrate that the things they were discussing in class were the things that people were discussing at the top universities. They appreciated that, too.

Though not every student loved every text, by overhauling the reading list and creating a new syllabus that reflected a variety of different themes, voices, and styles, students were exposed to a plethora of choices for reading—something they'd never had before. That was also appreciated.

Turns out it works. That year and those subsequent to it have taught us over and over again that it doesn't matter who is in the room. What matters are the teacher's high expectations and thoughtful assessment. What matters is how you create a dynamic classroom when talking about books. And frankly, what matters is a thoughtful consideration of which texts offer powerful voice, complex ideas, and good storytelling.

A word about student population. We are International Baccalaureate–trained teachers. IB is a program renowned for its rigor and high expectations, but we have also taught non-IB college prep courses, English language learner courses, and intervention courses.

By reevaluating our delivery of instruction and the content used, students in those courses have been extremely successful. They weren't going to become critical readers by reading travel brochures, as prescribed by some of the curriculum designed for them, but they did become better readers when given quality literature that was worthy of discussion.

In short, it shouldn't matter who your student population is. You tailor your delivery to the students in the room, but that doesn't mean you should condescend to your audience. They may do the work, but they won't love it, and if we want them to be hungry for success, they have to believe in what they are doing.

We were fortunate to begin our teaching careers in a magnet program in which we were expected to design our own rigorous curriculum centered on literary works and designed to prepare students for rigorous essay-based exams. Meanwhile, many of our colleagues were held to the demands of state- or district-mandated pacing guides and standardized testing schedules, with little room for rigorous curriculum design by individual teachers.

With the onset of Common Core, with its emphasis on critical thinking and logically developed writing, we thought we might have some relevant experience to share. What follows is a breakdown of how we approached our English classes. Everything in this book we've used. Everything in this book we created. We believe that if English teachers would take up this challenge, allow this core class that all students are required to take to be a lot tougher, a lot more rigorous, with a lot more writing, and if they would use good books—not just what they like, but good, quality, art—what we would have are scholars who (even if they aren't bound to be English majors) will appreciate the choices artists make, and will be happy to discuss those choices with you.

Acknowledgments

When we started this project together, we weren't sure anyone would ever read the finished product. It is an honor to have the Rowman & Littlefield team support our ideas and vision for what an English classroom could look like. In particular, we would like to thank our editor, Sarah Jubar, for believing in the book from the start and for taking so much time and putting forth so much energy to make sure it was as good as it possibly could be. The book simply wouldn't have happened without her.

A number of people have been instrumental in making this book happen. First of all, thanks to Ellen Old and Susan Halseth for their love, support, and amazing editing prowess.

Thanks also to our history department counterparts and collaborators on so many cross-curricular projects: Kati Berninger and Kristina Schoch-Giannosa. We are indebted in particular to Kati, our history guru and hands-down the best teacher we know, for her care and guidance in the development of chapter 9 of this book.

Of the many hundreds of students we've had the pleasure of teaching over the years, we were able to highlight in this book the work of a few exemplary scholars. Thank you to T. G. Roberts, Stacia Hildebrand, Erika Mendez, Samara Smith, Princess Vongchanh, and Andrea Baeza for allowing us to use your work.

Finally, thank you to our sons, Tom and Sam, for letting us disappear to Starbucks every Sunday to write like mad. We missed you each and every time and are so thankful for our wild and wonderful boys.

Introduction

With the onset of Common Core curriculum and assessments in school districts all across America, there is concern, distrust, and anxiety everywhere. What will the tests look like? Who writes them? How can we get our English language learners, our below-grade-level students, our migrant populations, prepared to write logical, cohesive arguments across multiple academic disciplines?

Anxiety such as this in education tends to create the desire for *the answer*—the single thing (textbook, professional development, purchased magic curriculum) that is a perfect fit for all shapes and sizes of student demographic. Ten years in the business of education has shown us this is a fool's errand.

Instead, we offer this book. By no means is it *the single thing*, but its goal is to empower teachers across America to feel confident in designing their own rigorous lessons to prepare their students for what awaits them in testing season, in college, and in their careers.

Nothing in this text is prescriptive. There are no daily lesson plans to follow, nor will you find a single bubble test within. You know your students. You know where they are and where they need to go.

By sharing nine of our own successful units of study, we hope to offer examples of what could be. The key is to take what will work for you and your students, tweak what needs tweaking, and leave the rest. As we suggest over and over in this book, the key is keeping the bar high for students while finding ways to engage them in the study of reading, writing about, and speaking about great, transformative literature. How you get there should be up to you, the professional in the room.

Many of us have heard that Common Core will put more of an emphasis on nonfiction texts; that may be true, but that doesn't mean that the study of literature should give up any ground in the classroom. If anything, students are not reading nearly enough iconic literature in a typical high school experience. This book suggests a myriad of ways to incorporate the study of quality nonfiction texts so that they work in tandem with the literature of your classroom and enhance student appreciation of what that literature means for its audience. That way, students and teachers alike avoid the "biography unit" or the "reading for information unit," which too often can be stale and superficial.

Instead, this text features a variety of strategies and ideas to get students reading, researching, and writing far more than they've ever been expected to. It demonstrates the necessity of keeping the onus of student learning on the individual student and shows concrete ways to keep the students reaching and the teacher facilitating student learning.

Everything in this book we've used. Everything in this book we've created. The student examples are from real-life students enrolled at our Title 1, socioeconomically diverse school.

Our hope is that the reading of *Method to the Madness: A Common Core Guide to Creating Critical Thinkers through the Study of Literature* will encourage teachers to create their own rigorous, fast-paced curriculum that meets the needs of their students.

Each chapter begins with a unit question that could serve as the basis of your anticipatory set, as well as the anchor of each unit's exploration. Unit questions should be open ended, and non–content specific. They are there to demonstrate to students how each unit of study is directly applicable to their own lives.

Seven of the nine chapters deal with specific literary texts as examples of what *may* happen in your room, never what *must* happen. Each text allows for the study of specific English-language skills, while still allowing students to gain exposure to and appreciation for great art. However, you should choose which texts will work best in your syllabus. The skills covered are not content specific; rather, they are examples of how to choose quality literature that best demonstrates the academic skills in each unit.

More than anything else, what we propose is simply this: if you want students to become better readers and writers—no matter what skill level they are currently at—you must provide them with fascinating texts to read about, write about, and think about. You must never condescend to your audience by providing canned, excerpted, low-quality literature. Expectations must be high, quality must be good, and engagement must be personal. That's why you're reading this, right? You care. You are invested. This must be true for our students as well.

To that end, this text works as a compilation of units that directly addresses what the shift to Common Core will demand of our classrooms.

✍ From the "Note on range and student reading" included adjacent to the anchor standards for reading:

> *To become college and career ready, students must grapple with works of exceptional craft and thought whose range extends across genres, cultures, and centuries. Such works offer profound insights into the human condition and serve as models for students' own thinking and writing. Along with high-quality contemporary works, these texts should be chosen from among seminal U.S. documents, the classics of American literature, and the timeless dramas of Shakespeare.*

What follows are nine units of study that align themselves to the Common Core Anchor Standards for English Language Arts. We hope they will encourage you to create your own powerful units of study that can be transformative for you and your students.

Chapter One

Writing for Critical Thinking and Logical Cohesiveness (Or, How to Survive the Shift to Common Core)

This book is about reading, but we will begin with a chapter on writing. High-level writing will be the means by which high-level reading is assessed, and is the best way to assess the reading standards of the Common Core.

This chapter provides strategies for improving student writing, both through increased quality and increased quantity, without increasing the teacher's grading workload. It will include step-by-step instructions for how to move students toward frequent, high-level writing in multiple drafts, as well as how to manage the grading of that writing without giving up one's personal life (completely, anyway). The goal of the chapter is to help teachers make writing urgent for students as well as familiar, and to make writing assignments both relevant and rigorous.

COMMON CORE STANDARDS ADDRESSED

✍ Common Core College and Career Readiness Anchor Standards for Writing

1. Write arguments to support claims in an analysis of substantive topics or texts, using valid reasoning and relevant and sufficient evidence.

2. Write informative/explanatory texts to examine and convey complex ideas and information clearly and accurately through the effective selection, organization, and analysis of content.

4. Produce clear and coherent writing in which the development, organization, and style are appropriate to task, purpose, and audience.

5. Develop and strengthen writing as needed by planning, revising, editing, rewriting, or trying a new approach.

WHY STUDENTS MUST BE WRITING

One of the most glaring trends of the last ten years or so in the subject of English at the high school level is the low emphasis put on high-quality, inquiry-based writing. The state standardized exams were bubble tests. The high school exit exam had a single essay portion with incredibly low standards. Only the ACT, IB, and AP tests (all of which are geared toward college-bound students) put significant emphasis on whether students could write coherently, with logically developed arguments.

In many cases, this reveals that intensive writing units were sacrificed for the more immediate needs of the bubble tests. This doesn't mean English teachers aren't teaching writing, but they haven't been doing it enough (or haven't been *allowed* to do it enough) and with enough rigor, and students are graduating from high school having written too few papers. This contributes to a lack of confidence and comfort for students when it comes to their written voice.

Well, the joke is on us, because Common Core will expect students to be able to compose and support their thoughts in writing across all the academic disciplines. So how does one prepare them to do that?

STARTING OFF STRONG

Consider *beginning* your year with an intensive writing unit. Make this choice on the assumption that you will be having your students write every day, every week, and it will be easier to lay the foundation early.

Many schools experience high student turnover in the first quarter—kids moving in and out of classes. In such a case, consider making a writing folder complete with notes, handouts, and annotated student exemplars available for students as they enter your class. Despite the chaos of a situation like that, the class must be able to always move forward with rigor. New skills must be introduced.

The additional benefit of placing this unit at the beginning of your year is that it allows you to subsequently dive into your first text without having to pause for days or weeks to reteach basic skills and expectations. By your front-loading one of the most fundamental skills of the subject (writing coherently for an audience), the students will naturally apply that skill to all subsequent units of study and be additionally prepared for their end-of-year Common Core assessments.

CHANGING THE GAME: HOW TO INCORPORATE MORE WRITING

Quantity of Writing

Do a *lot* of writing. Do an absurd amount of writing in your class. There should be papers, but there should also be speeches and debates accompanied by notes and reflections and creative writing and annotating song lyrics and more. People get better at something by doing it a lot. Therefore, teachers need to provide ample opportunity for practice. When this idea is broached to a room full of teachers, they will always want to know, "How do you keep up with the grading?" Well, see the following.

Grading Practices

Don't always tell your students what you will grade. A teacher once said to us, "If you're grading everything they are writing, they aren't writing enough." It's true. Students don't need to know that. They need to know that you have assigned writing assignments that they are expected to complete. You are still providing practice but are also creating an environment in which you as the teacher can have success as well. And if you grade everything, it doesn't really matter, does it? This is not to suggest that what you grade should become arbitrary or conditional; rather, there are strategies to focus the grading of writing assignments to make it more manageable.

Think of it this way: when you are on a team, no one watches you practice at home, right? But the practice will lead to more success on game day. Students need to buy into the need to *practice* their writing. This is more effective if the practice clearly leads to success on "game day" in your class. This chapter will discuss some scenarios that keep students writing and allow time for you to focus on providing timely, quality feedback on that writing.

Scenario for Student Practice and Teacher Success

For example, in one week during a unit on *The Great Gatsby*, students may be working on an individual process paper with the prompt, "Discuss color symbolism in the novel and its effect." They've done a rough draft, received feedback, and at home they are finishing their final draft. The teacher will only grade the final draft.

But that week in class, students are also preparing a debate (the topic of which is "Gatsby is the villain in the text"), and teams are preparing notes using textual evidence in class. They must have the notes to do well in the debate, but the teacher won't collect the notes for a grade.

Also, each class session will begin with a five-minute timed writing—a one-page minimum response on the following prompts:

Monday: Why does Fitzgerald include the character Wolfsheim? What does it accomplish?
Tuesday: How does the character Owl Eyes help us to understand Gatsby more deeply?
Wednesday: Why is it important that Nick is an unreliable narrator?
Thursday: After reading the bathroom scene, do you blame Daisy for marrying Tom ?
Friday: Discuss your thoughts on yesterday's debate.

By Friday, students have created seven to ten pages of new writing, but which is to be graded? Maybe the debate notes or timed writing is credit/no credit. Maybe you collect the timed writing and choose six randomly to spot-check their understanding.

But you probably don't grade them all. Not every week. Because how many of us can get through all those papers and provide useful feedback in a timely manner?

However, by pacing a single week this way, students have had to respond coherently, and in writing, *seven times* in English class that week, and of these assignments, only one (the final draft of the color-symbolism process essay) will be formally graded.

Additionally, each of these assignments has been pertinent to their understanding of the lessons that week, has deepened their understanding of the literary text, and has forced them to engage interactively with the text. They have also practiced writing in a variety of ways (timed writing, textual evidence and notes for a debate, a process paper with a rough and final draft).

Because they are practicing responding to such questions about the text and preparing for debates, their analytical papers due on Friday will be better. They've been practicing. Each assessment allows rigorous, realistic practice for your entire student body but does *not* necessitate laboriously grading everything produced.

Students will do the work because the practice leads them to the two major assessments of the week: their final paper and their group debate. They won't even notice that they've spent the week doing three times the amount of practice than will ultimately be graded, but they will benefit from it nevertheless.

Don't Always Grade the Whole Paper

When grading, do not always grade the whole paper. Wait! This step only works if:

- Your expectations are consistently high, and your students know that.
- You *do* regularly grade a paper in its entirety, looking for development, persuasiveness, appropriate evidence, and more.

However, two or three times a year when dealing with a full process, multi-draft paper, employ this technique. Students must believe that this paper will matter. It will need to be a major portion of their grade. Tell the students it will only be graded on two things:

1. the quality of their thesis statement and . . .
2. *one* randomly chosen body paragraph. That's it. They won't know which body paragraph will be chosen, and it won't matter if the rest of their paper is magnificent.

Why is this so effective?

- You are spending less time grading and more time setting expectations for your students.
- Your students are looking much more closely at the usefulness and effectiveness of *every word* of every body paragraph—they are reflecting on their own writing because the stakes are higher.
- It makes students focus on developing a clear, unmistakable connection between their thesis and every word of their paper.

The benefits here are pretty noteworthy. The technique will also reap rewards at the end of the year when students are writing their independent responses for their Common Core assessments. They'll understand the importance of a strong thesis and articulate support throughout their argument, and they'll be accustomed to editing and revising their own work independently. This strategy has been hugely helpful in making believers of students in the importance of a quality thesis as well as the mantra, "If it doesn't support your thesis, you don't need it."

However, don't do it all the time. That isn't fair to the student. It is important that all body paragraphs work together, that the evidence build, and that the conclusion progress logically from the body, but this is a great way to get another process paper in without it slowing down the class's momentum with grading. How many of us have provided fastidious feedback, but it took us weeks to get marked papers back to students? Timeliness matters in grading. Remember, *if you are grading everything they are writing, they aren't writing enough.*

CREATING URGENCY

A classroom should always feel urgent. Students must believe it is important to do the work asked of them. This means the teacher must *only* assign tasks that authentically build upon one another, and "fillers" (worksheets, etc.) must be kept to a bare minimum. In order to ensure success with any strategy in the classroom, the goal of the teacher should always be to make writing urgent for the student, and to make writing common for the student.

Strategies to Create Urgency about Writing

- Hand students a slip of paper as they come in for class—they are expected to immediately start answering a posted prompt *before* the bell rings.
- Set a time limit for quick writes at the start of class that establishes urgency. For instance, one full page in four minutes—this way, students are writing with urgency, trying to reach the goal; they are striving intensely, instead of passively participating.
- Make sure in-class activities and outside-class activities (homework, essay writing) reflect one another. For instance, students should bring their rough drafts to class (which are worth points) so that they can participate in an intensive peer-edit process (which is worth *more* points than the rough draft). The writing they do needs to matter on multiple fronts. The goal is to always establish that the *practice* of writing will benefit them both immediately and in the long term.

TEACHING THE BONES OF ESSAY CONSTRUCTION

If it is necessary to teach your class the basics of essay construction, begin with a very basic series of lessons on the five-paragraph essay. Tell students (no matter what level they are at) that five paragraphs may be too short to prove a point sufficiently, that you are merely teaching them the bones of the writing process, and that additional and more complex "meat" should continuously be added to those bones. What follows are the very basics for getting started crafting essays.

Note: each of these essay "bones" needs to be taught in class explicitly by the instructor, with opportunities to practice each step before a student should be graded on an entire essay. Your unit plan needs to allow for time to perform a pre-assessment where you can gauge how much of the essay structure has already been mastered by the majority of the students in the room, as well as for time to directly teach the basics if necessary. Allow at least two to three days for this.

Titles

The title of an essay should be engaging, and not a cliché. Titling an essay "Essay" should not be sufficient, nor should "Characterization Essay."

Activity—Title Competition

A good practice activity here is a small-group competition. As a whole group, read an essay, but don't tell students the title of the essay. This can be something of your creation or a student example.

Then, give groups five minutes to come up with the best, most dynamic title for the paper they've just read. Have them share out, with emphasis on explaining *why* they chose what they chose and how it reflects the purpose of the essay, followed by a class vote on the best title.

Introduction

In the beginning, students may still use a hook—especially if the class is at a lower grade level. As the skill level increases, token tricks and formulas should be discouraged. These things are a place to start, not a place to land. However, in the beginning of the year, such strategies can be useful.

The last sentence of the introduction paragraph should be the thesis statement. Spend most of your time on the thesis statement. If they understand that, the rest will come.

The Rules of the Thesis Statement

Rule one: No fence sitting. No "I think" or "maybe." These weaken the argument and make it seem as if the idea isn't worthy of discussion. It will help if you make "I" a prohibited word in their writing, at least until they can negotiate it academically.

Rule two: The thesis must have an opposite side to argue. For example, "Holden Caulfield is no longer interesting to the current generation of American students" is declarative, but it can also be argued against, in scholarly debate.

Rule Three: The thesis must be analytical. No obvious statements. A thesis must suggest that the student has read or studied something and has an original idea about the content worth arguing about. An unacceptable thesis is something like, "Holden Caulfield is unsatisfied." That is declarative, and technically an argument, but it is obvious and doesn't prove that the student thought about the text. It doesn't add anything to the conversation. That isn't allowed.

Body Paragraphs

There are two vital ingredients to an effective body paragraph: a topic sentence and supporting evidence.

Topic Sentence

First of all, body paragraphs must always begin with an analytical topic sentence that supports *one aspect* of the declarative thesis statement. They must clearly be related to the thesis. No new information can be introduced.

To demonstrate, let's stay with our discussion of Holden Caulfield.

Thesis Statement: Holden Caulfield is no longer interesting to the current generation of American students.

Topic Sentence One: Holden's vernacular is outdated.

Topic Sentence Two: Holden's internal conflicts are too ambiguous and lack real urgency.

Topic Sentence Three: Despite Holden's popularity with previous generations, it is no longer revolutionary to encounter an aloof, disenchanted voice in media.

Each of these clearly supports the thesis but also offers independent analytical reasons *why* the thesis is correct. Additionally, each of these topic sentences demonstrates an engaged, analytical reading of the text. Students are not reporting what happens in a text; rather, they are adding something new to the fifty-year-old conversation of Holden Caulfield's characterization and its impact.

Supporting Evidence

Body paragraphs should always include evidence from the text. This evidence should be embedded naturally within the body of the paragraph. Teach students to avoid plugging in ineffective evidence; instead, evidence should support *their* ideas and *their* analysis.

Conclusion

A conclusion should not restate what was already said. A conclusion should leave the reader with the impression that they should want to know more and that the topic of the paper really matters. Students should assume that their audience has understood the thesis, so to merely repeat it is redundant and, therefore, useless. Rather, a good conclusion should aim at creating further curiosity about the topic in the reader.

Taking It Further

Once students get these bones, it is time to start layering on. Students who haven't written very much have trouble pushing their writing deeper, taking time to fully examine and discuss their analysis. It is the student instinct to say something and move on. This habit must be broken. Their writing needs to be more reflective.

Teachers should build in time to layer "meat" onto this process, like style, voice, irony, and more. These are the things that almost never get taught. Students are taught year after year the same formula that any good writer would balk at—such strategies can only be an initial tool. And if the students already have it mastered, then move on to cultivating their individual written voice.

INCORPORATING QUALITY PRACTICE IN WRITING

We've already discussed raising the quantity of writing in English classes. Now let's discuss how we can incorporate writing practice that is of a high quality.

What follows is a weeklong scenario. Each day focuses on a distinct facet of the writing process while simultaneously allowing students to see how the writing process builds upon itself. Additionally, student and teacher alike are spending the week interacting with literature *while practicing the appropriate skills.* The study of literature never stops in order for us to teach or reteach writing.

Day One: Have students enter the room and receive a timed-writing prompt. Let's say it is based on your class's study of *Macbeth.* The prompt for the day is, "Discuss Shakespeare's use of women in the play." They have one hour to compose an essay that shows:

- structure;
- a persuasive, compelling thesis;
- evidence from the text; and

- evidence of their study of the text (notes, independent research, their thoughts, and so on.

These papers are not going to be perfect by the end of the hour. They may not even be finished. However, you have already created *urgency* with the imposed time limit. Consider letting them use both their texts and their notes during the process to anchor their responses. But by the end of the hour, students will not have a finished product. They'll have a beginning of a product. You, and they, can't be finished yet.

Day Two: Peruse the papers and choose one or two to use as your exemplars. Choose middle-of-the-road papers—papers where the good and the bad are apparent. During the next class, project these papers (sans student names) for all to see. Put the students in small groups (or not—you know your students) and lead a class discussion on what works and what doesn't within the student example. Here are some questions to ask:

- Is there a clear thesis that meets all the qualifications?
- Does each topic sentence help organize the argument for the thesis?
- Do the body paragraphs logically and specifically support the thesis?
- Is the evidence compelling?
- Does the argument logically progress toward the conclusion articulately and persuasively?

By the end of the hour, tell the students they have *only that night* to finish their rough drafts—they haven't been graded yet. Tomorrow, when they walk in, you're choosing three at random to call on and projecting their papers. Those drafts, due tomorrow, will be graded.

We have already created urgency without compromising rigor and critical thinking because:

- The prompt is accessible, but sophisticated.
- They were able to use their resources for their initial draft.
- They were able to work in small groups or in a whole-class conversation about what works in papers and what doesn't.
- Students who were really struggling will have seen student examples (remember, middle-of-the road examples, not your shining stars) to help them get started, as well as the benefit of their peers' observations.
- They had the prompt for three days before the first graded draft was done.
- They know they may have to share their papers tomorrow, not anonymously, which will create urgency to do the best they can with a draft that they've had days to think about with lots of support.

Will all these drafts be perfect? No. Will they be *so much better* than if you graded them after the initial timed writing? Yes!

Day Three: Collect papers on day three of the process. Remember, it's just a first draft. The next level of intervention is you.

If you are swamped with grading, consider choosing one-third of the papers, and read them through while making a tally list of common problems with that third of the class. Take all papers back to the students, discuss common problems, and use that list of common problems for your lesson plan for the next one to two days.

Days Four and Five: Did that third of the class demonstrate that they are using weak theses? That needs work-shopping. Are they improperly quoting the text? That needs work-shopping. Are their conclusions boring and repetitive? That needs work-shopping. Spend the next two days reviewing the rules for common problems you're seeing.

After they've had a refresher course, ask students, "After these lessons, who needs to take their draft back and make adjustments?" The vast majority will come up and grab their paper. Give them that day in class to handwrite the corrections or additions, or give it as homework (if your students can be trusted to bring it back the next day).

Then, when it is as good as it can possibly be by *only them*, you grade and edit that draft. That's where you give feedback, both positive and negative. But that feedback means so much more because they've been working with this paper for over a week.

SO WHAT?—AND HOW IT CHANGES EVERYTHING

The simple question "So what?" becomes everything to you and your student. When providing feedback, underline a vague phrase, a quote that doesn't add anything to the argument, and write, in big letters, SO WHAT? And then make students answer you.

Activity—The "So What?" Sign

When students are standing up in front of the class giving an oral response, have the phrase "So What?" written in Sharpie on a piece of paper or cardboard and hold it up from the back of the room. It will become an inside joke by the end of the year, but it will also *force* them to acknowledge that their argument isn't done yet. It will force them to dig deeper. This doesn't sound like much, but it is the difference between a thoughtful, reflective writer (and perhaps person?) and not.

Activity—Listening for the "So What?"

If your students become comfortable enough, create situations in which student panels grade group presentations. Have them use the "So what?" sign. They'll amaze you with their ability to *hear* a weak, underdeveloped argument before too long. This is great practice, because it should be coming from them, as you work with them. Their ability to hear a weak argument and edit it in the moment is the goal. A little voice in their head that sounds like your angry pen in the margins saying "So what? You haven't said anything yet!" And then, success.

The most important takeaway with this strategy is this: don't settle for noise after you ask a student, "So what?." Keep asking them, "So what?" until you get a quality reflective response. For example:

> Student: *The Grapes of Wrath* often uses biblical imagery to create symbolism.
>
> Teacher: So what?
>
> Student: The biblical imagery adds importance to our understanding of the symbolism in the text.
>
> Teacher: So what?
>
> Student: This is important because the purposeful juxtaposition of biblical imagery and symbolism allows the audience to infer that the Joads and the other Okies are aligned with the Bible.
>
> Teacher: So what?
>
> Student: This juxtaposition lets us infer that the Okies are to be sympathized with, which is important because this is a piece of muckraker fiction. Our sympathy aligned with the Joads would encourage the audience to take action to better the plight of all emigrating people.

It might not come across that articulately or cleanly, but because the teacher pushed repeatedly, the student (and the audience of students waiting their turn) come to understand that one strong, analytical statement is not the finish line. Instead, they come to understand that everything they say should be interconnected and supported to create a more effective argument.

When introducing this to your classroom, make sure you can accomplish two things simultaneously:

- You can keep your expectations high and *wait* until you have a quality response before moving on, and . . .
- You can hold the line while supporting the student. This isn't a tactic to pick on them. Rather, it needs to be delivered in a way that teaches them

how to hear the weakness in their *own* arguments. Be supportive, and insist that peers in the class are also being supportive. Otherwise, students will clam up, and you'll get nowhere fast.

By using the "So what?" tool consistently, your students will be better prepared to edit and revise their Common Core written responses. There is no checklist or worksheet involved with this exercise. The teacher puts the onus of the quality of the response on the student—over and over again. The student realizes they know the answer; they have just failed to put all the pieces together in one place. The result is that all answers (in written or oral form) will be more reflective and more interconnected and will show more depth of understanding.

SUMMARY

This chapter has demonstrated the importance of crafting writing units that create opportunities for authentic practice in writing. Teachers should never feel as though they can't have students constantly writing because they can't keep up with the grading—*if you are grading everything they are writing, they aren't writing enough.*

For success in Common Core assessments—and in college and career—move students toward critical thinking, analysis, and critical writing. These should be the tenets you use while teaching writing to your students *without* sacrificing simultaneous study of complex literary texts.

Chapter Two

Begin with Close Reading

UNIT QUESTION: SO WHAT?

INTRODUCTION

Teaching students to read analytically—to "close read"—is to teach students to be aware of and to appreciate *choices* made by the author or poet.

Students should practice looking at all elements of a text—word choice, word placement, patterns, repetitions, punctuation, and so on—as potentially a conscious choice that is significant and worth further discussion (not only *identify* choices, but consider the *effect* of those choices). Students should also be given a "language" with which to identify (be aware of) and discuss the effect of (appreciate) these choices. This language, for the most part, will consist of what are typically referred to as "literary terms."

It is important to note here, with the risk of being repetitive, that when close reading, students should be able to not only *identify* choices but to also consider the *effect* of the choice. In other words, students should practice answering the question, "So what?"

Common Core assessments will require constructed student responses in paragraph or short-essay form. It is therefore essential that we prepare students to move past merely identifying aspects of literature and toward being comfortable navigating and interacting confidently with unfamiliar, sometimes intimidating pieces of text. Students must independently meet a new text and have a skill set for examining the purpose behind its author's choices.

This is not easy. It is also, quite often, very different from what students may have been expected to do in previous English courses. Therefore, students being taught to close read should be provided with substantial support and practice, and it is a good idea to start small.

Activity—Introducing Close Reading

What follows is a lesson that introduces students to analyzing literature through close reading.

✍ This particular lesson addresses two of the ten Common Core College and Career Readiness Anchor Standards for 6th to 12th Grade Reading:

1. Read closely to determine what the text says explicitly and to make logical inferences from it; cite specific textual evidence when writing or speaking to support conclusions drawn from the text.

4. Interpret words and phrases as they are used in a text, including determining technical, connotative, and figurative meanings, and analyze how specific word choices shape meaning or tone.

A possible place to begin is with a passage such as the following, which is the opening paragraph of Edgar Allan Poe's short story, "The Fall of the House of Usher."

> *DURING the whole of a dull, dark, and soundless day in the autumn of the year, when the clouds hung oppressively low in the heavens, I had been passing alone, on horseback, through a singularly dreary tract of country; and at length found myself, as the shades of the evening drew on, within view of the melancholy House of Usher. I know not how it was—but, with the first glimpse of the building, a sense of insufferable gloom pervaded my spirit. I say insufferable; for the feeling was unrelieved by any of that half-pleasurable, because poetic, sentiment, with which the mind usually receives even the sternest natural images of the desolate or terrible. I looked upon the scene before me—upon the mere house, and the simple landscape features of the domain—upon the bleak walls—upon the vacant eye-like windows—upon a few rank sedges—and upon a few white trunks of decayed trees—with an utter depression of soul which I can compare to no earthly sensation more properly than to the after-dream of the reveller upon opium—the bitter lapse into everyday life—the hideous dropping off of the veil. There was an iciness, a sinking, a sickening of the heart—an unredeemed dreariness of thought which no goading of the imagination could torture into aught of the sublime. What was it—I paused to think—what was it that so unnerved me in the contemplation of the House of Usher?*

The passage, though short and therefore manageable, is rich with opportunities for analysis, and is one we have used numerous times in numerous lessons over the years.

As mentioned, students will first need some language with which to approach the passage. For this particular lesson, the following will do:

- Diction: word choice
- Imagery: phrases that create an image in the reader's mind
- Mood: the feeling—or atmosphere—of a piece of writing

Students should understand that, when close reading, we talk about the "big" things by talking about the "little" things. In other words, we discuss the big, abstract ideas by focusing on the effect of the small, concrete details on the page.

One way to explain this to students is to say that we can't concretely point to the "big," or abstract (such as theme), on the page, but we can point on the page to the specific details, or *choices* (such as a metaphor), that work to develop those big ideas.

Activity—Finding the Mood

In this lesson, we will be examining the mood (big idea) of the passage by analyzing Poe's diction and imagery (small details). The aim of this lesson is to develop an appreciation of the interconnectedness of all literary terms once they are applied. Students will begin to see that these words are not a list to memorize, but rather that they build upon one another. Imagery begets mood, which begets foreshadowing, which begets symbolism, and so on.

The first step in this lesson is to read the passage, which should probably be first read by the teacher, given the difficulty and/or unfamiliarity of some of the language.

After reading, ask the class, "What is the story/passage's *mood*?" Or you can ask the students to first tell their neighbor what the mood is, and then ask the whole class. Students are usually familiar enough, from other contexts, with the concept of "mood," but if students are struggling, ask, "What's the "feel" of the story?" Student responses should range from *dark* or *sad* or *scary* to *depression* or *anxiety* or *despair*. For English language learners, the teacher can increase the likelihood of students picking up on this mood with a little extra "performance" in the initial reading.

By listing responses on the board, the class should be able to come to a consensus as to the passage's mood. Varying student skill levels should not be an issue here, as a low-level descriptor (such as *sad*) will work just as well as a higher-level descriptor (such as *depressed*).

Let's say the class has decided that the passage gives off a *depressed* mood. The next step will be for the teacher to read the passage aloud a second time.

DURING the whole of a dull, dark, and soundless day in the autumn of the year, when the clouds hung oppressively low in the heavens, I had been passing alone, on horseback, through a singularly dreary tract of country; and at length found myself, as the shades of the evening drew on, within view of the melancholy House of Usher. I know not how it was—but, with the first glimpse of the building, a sense of insufferable gloom pervaded my spirit. I say insufferable; for the feeling was unrelieved by any of that half-pleasurable, because poetic, sentiment, with which the mind usually receives even the sternest natural images of the desolate or terrible. I looked upon the scene before me—upon the mere house, and the simple landscape features of the domain—upon the bleak walls—upon the vacant eye-like windows—upon a few rank sedges—and upon a few white trunks of decayed trees—with an utter depression of soul which I can compare to no earthly sensation more properly than to the after-dream of the reveller upon opium—the bitter lapse into everyday life—the hideous dropping off of the veil. There was an iciness, a sinking, a sickening of the heart—an unredeemed dreariness of thought which no goading of the imagination could torture into aught of the sublime. What was it—I paused to think—what was it that so unnerved me in the contemplation of the House of Usher?

This time, students will be instructed to follow along and circle or highlight any word that they feel helps to create the "depressed" mood. The result will probably look a lot like textbox 2.1.

Students should then discuss with their neighbor the diction that they identified, after which a "whole class" list should be written on the board. Discussion can be held as to how or why particular pieces of diction contribute to the mood. For example, the instructor should push for an answer as to why the diction of "torture" demonstrates a depressed mood. This could lead to a conversation about inference and connotation, additional literary terms. The goal should be to create articulated responses as to why particular examples of diction contribute to the mood of the piece. Identification of the diction is only the first step.

Activity—Finding the Imagery

The process just described will then be repeated, this time with the focus on *imagery* as opposed to diction. As the teacher rereads the passage (or pairs reread it together), students will be underlining groups of words that create an image (either visual, auditory, olfactory, gustatory, or tactile) that help to *create* the depressed mood. Students should again share with their neighbor, followed by the whole group. The result may look something like textbox 2.2 (imagery words or phrases are underlined):

Again, students should recognize from this activity how diction and imagery can contribute to the mood of a piece of literature.

DURING the whole of a <u>dull, dark, and soundless day</u> in the autumn of the year, when the <u>clouds hung oppressively low in the heavens,</u> I had been passing <u>alone, on horseback,</u> through a singularly <u>dreary tract of country;</u> and at length found myself, as the shades of the evening drew on, within view of the melancholy House of Usher. I know not how it was—but, with the first glimpse of the building, a sense of insufferable gloom pervaded my spirit. I say insufferable; for the feeling was unrelieved by any of that half-pleasurable, because poetic, sentiment, with which the mind usually receives even the sternest natural images of the desolate or terrible. I looked upon the scene before me—upon the mere house, and the simple landscape features of the domain—upon <u>the bleak walls</u>—upon <u>the vacant eye-like windows</u>—upon <u>a few rank sedges</u>—and upon <u>a few white trunks of decayed trees</u>—with an utter depression of soul which I can compare to no earthly sensation more properly than to the after-dream of the reveller upon opium—the bitter lapse into everyday life—<u>the hideous dropping off of the veil</u>. There was an iciness, a sinking, a sickening of the heart—an unredeemed dreariness of thought which no goading of the imagination could torture into aught of the sublime. What was it—I paused to think—what was it that so unnerved me in the contemplation of the House of Usher?

Activity—A Close Read on a Cold Read

The next step in the lesson is for students to demonstrate their ability to do this on their own, which will require an additional passage to analyze. Suitable passages for close reading can be found in a variety of texts; for example, Harper Lee's description of Maycomb County in chapter 1 of *To Kill a Mockingbird,* or the turtle vignette in John Steinbeck's *The Grapes of Wrath.* Whichever passage you choose, make sure that it includes significant authorial choices about which students can make inferences.

Once you have chosen a passage, break the students into groups. In pairs or small groups, students should identify and list:

- The mood of the passage
- Diction that helps to create the mood
- Images that help to create the mood

The final "product" of this lesson should be a paragraph—written in class or at home—discussing the mood of the passage and what creates that mood. This paragraph will require students to support their claim (the mood) with textual evidence (specific diction and imagery), which is a foundational writing skill in the Common Core Standards, specifically College and Career Readiness Anchor Standard for Writing #1.

✍ *CCRW6–12.1 Write arguments to support claims in an analysis of substantive topics or texts, using valid reasoning and relevant and sufficient evidence.*

After working with these passages, students will have begun to annotate an unfamiliar text and will have been introduced to the practice of focusing on details (choices) and their larger effect. The passages suggested here can of course be replaced by others, but it is worth noting that "opening" passages tend to work well for this lesson.

Activity—The Power of "Sticks"

Once students have mastered the basics of close reading, they are ready to recognize and to analyze (appreciate the effects of) a wider range of authorial choices. They are also ready to add vocabulary to the "language" that they use to discuss those choices.

A strategy that never fails in the classroom is the use of George Saunders's two-paragraph short story "Sticks." It is simple, elegant, purposeful, and accessible to students of all abilities and makes for a great "next step" in helping students to master close reading.

Here's the story. Again, it's only two paragraphs:

Sticks

by George Saunders

Every year Thanksgiving night we flocked out behind Dad as he dragged the Santa suit to the road and draped it over a kind of crucifix he'd built out of a metal pole in the yard. Super Bowl week the pole was dressed in a jersey and Rod's helmet and Rod had to clear it with Dad if he wanted to take the helmet off. On the Fourth of July the pole was Uncle Sam, on Veteran's Day a soldier, on Halloween a ghost. The pole was Dad's only concession to glee. We were allowed a single Crayola from the box at a time. One Christmas Eve he shrieked at Kimmie for wasting an apple slice. He hovered over us as we poured ketchup saying: good enough good enough good enough. Birthday parties consisted of cupcakes, no ice cream. The first time I brought a date over she said: what's with your dad and that pole? and I sat there blinking.

We left home, married, had children of our own, found the seeds of meanness blooming also within us. Dad began dressing the pole with more complexity and less discernible logic. He draped some kind of fur over it on Groundhog Day and lugged out a floodlight to ensure a shadow. When an earthquake struck Chile he lay the pole on its side and spray painted a rift in the earth. Mom died and he dressed the pole as Death and hung from the crossbar photos of Mom as a baby. We'd stop by and find odd talismans from his youth arranged around the base: army medals, theater tickets, old sweatshirts, tubes of Mom's makeup. One autumn he painted the pole bright yellow. He covered it with cotton swabs that winter for warmth and provided offspring by hammering in six crossed sticks around the yard. He ran lengths of string between the pole and the sticks, and taped to the string letters of apology, admissions of error, pleas for understanding, all written in a frantic hand on index cards. He painted a sign saying LOVE and hung it from the pole and another that said FORGIVE? and then he died in the hall with the radio on and we sold the house to a young couple who yanked out the pole and the sticks and left them by the road on garbage day.

It's a short yet dense story that appeals to students of all backgrounds and abilities. It's close to magic.

This story can be used in a variety of ways to teach a variety of skills. For example, it can be used to analyze the effect of concrete details ("showing" Dad to the readers, through concrete detail, rather than "telling"). It can also be used to analyze conflict in fiction. Students could debate who or what the protagonist of the story is, likewise the antagonist, and thereby what the actual conflict is (the answers to these questions are more complex than you may think). Another possibility is to use the story specifically to teach the concept of "inference."

What follows is a lesson that uses "Sticks" to teach close reading in general. This lesson would naturally follow the lesson described in "Introducing Close Reading."

Let's begin by expanding our literary terms list, to which we've already added *diction*, *imagery*, and *mood*.

Explicit: direct; straightforward
Implicit: suggested; hinted at
Inference: a "guess" based on what is implied in the text
Diction: specific word choice
Denotation: the explicit meaning of a word
Connotation: the implicit meaning of a word
Imagery: phrases that create an image in the reader's mind
Figurative Language: description through comparison
Simile: an explicit comparison
Metaphor: an implicit comparison
Personification: a metaphor in which human characteristics are assigned to something nonhuman.
Mood: the feeling—or atmosphere—of a piece of writing
Tone: the attitude of a piece of writing
Characterization: what an author shows or tells us about a character
Direct Characterization: what an author explicitly tells us about a character
Indirect Characterization: what an author implicitly shows us about a character
Theme: a universal idea
Motif: a pattern of repeated images (three or more is a pattern)
Allusion: a reference to something well-known from literature, mythology, history, or religion
Irony: a gap between what happens and what is expected
Juxtaposition: the placement of two things side-by-side for a particular effect
Conflict: what the protagonist wants and the reason they can't have it
Protagonist: the character that struggles against the conflict
Antagonist: the person or thing that gets in the way of what the protagonist wants
Resolution: the solution to the conflict

You may need to modify this list for your grade level and the specific skills being taught, but this is a pretty basic list of literary terms students should be able to use. The first two or three days of this lesson are devoted to learning the terms, which can be achieved through group work, games, quizzes, or all of the above. Bottom line: students need to be familiar with their literary terms.

Once these terms are learned, at a basic level, it is time to roll out "Sticks." Pass it out, and read it aloud so the first reading provides inflection and tone for the students. Then—in small groups or individually—students will annotate the story (which they have begun to do with their previous practice passages). The teacher or the students, depending on their comfort level, can guide this activity. The instructions for annotating the text can be as simple as follows: "Use your pens and highlighters to mark words and phrases in the text that you find significant. In the margins, briefly note the significance of the word or phrase. In your margin notes, try to use your literary terms."

It may be a good idea, the first time, to do this together. A document camera or overhead projector can be used to display the story, and the whole class can annotate the story together. The extent to which this annotation is directed by the teacher or by the students will depend entirely on the class, and you should get a feel for where they are right away.

For a more advanced class, the story can be annotated in small groups, and as you wander through the groups, you should get a good sense of how comfortable they are applying terms to a new text. When this is done, guide a discussion of the annotations with the class. What they found, where, and why it matters. This is a great time to reinforce the essential question, *So what*? Remember, it is not enough for students to *identify* choices, they must also appreciate the *effects* of those choices.

Figures 2.1 and 2.2 represent sample annotations. A teacher annotated figure 2.1 as an exemplar to give to students *after* they've given it a whirl independently. A tenth-grade student completed the second annotation, figure 2.2. These student attempts at annotation should be a beginning, not an end. Check what they did when they were on their own, but as a large group, push to make connections more thorough and connect multiple pieces of textual evidence to one term. For instance, the father's dialogue in the first paragraph can be annotated separately, but, together, it provides a clear characterization of the father and establishes a clear mood.

Taking It Further

If you are satisfied that the annotations and discussions prove that students are adequately interacting with the text, have them write a short paper on how authorial choice in Saunders's "Sticks" effects audience understanding of the story.

Sticks

by George Saunders.

Every year Thanksgiving night we flocked out behind Dad as he dragged the Santa suit to the road and draped it over a kind of crucifix he'd built out of a metal pole in the yard. Super Bowl week the pole was dressed in a jersey and Rod's helmet and Rod had to clear it with Dad if he wanted to take the helmet off. On the Fourth of July the pole was Uncle Sam, on Veterans' Day a soldier, on Halloween a ghost. The pole was Dad's only concession to glee. We were allowed a single Crayola from the box at a time. One Christmas Eve he shrieked at Kimmie for wasting an apple slice. He hovered over us as we poured ketchup saying: good enough good enough good enough. Birthday parties consisted of cupcakes, no ice cream. The first I brought a date over she said: what's with your dad and that pole? and I sat there blinking.

We left home, married, had children of our own, found the seeds of meanness blooming also within us. Dad began dressing the pole with more complexity and less discernible logic. He draped some kind of fur over it on Groundhog Day and lugged out a floodlight to ensure a shadow. When an earthquake struck Chile he laid the pole on its side and spray painted a rift in the earth. Mom died and he dressed the pole as Death and hung from the crossbar photos of Mom as a baby. We'd stop by and find odd talismans from his youth arranged around the base: army medals, theater tickets, old sweatshirts, tubes of Mom's makeup. One autumn he painted the pole bright yellow. He covered it with cotton swabs that winter for warmth and provided offspring by hammering in six crossed sticks around the yard. He ran lengths of string between the pole and the sticks, and taped to the string letters of apology, admissions of error, pleas for understanding, all written in a frantic hand on index cards. He painted a sign saying LOVE and hung it from the pole and another that said FORGIVE? and then he died in the hall with the radio on and we sold the house to a young couple who yanked out the pole and the sticks and left them by the road on garbage day.

Figure 2.1.

Sticks

by George Saunders.

Every year Thanksgiving night we flocked out behind Dad as he dragged the Santa suit to the road and draped it over a kind of crucifix he'd built out of a metal pole in the yard. Super Bowl week the pole was dressed in a jersey and Rod's helmet and Rod had to clear it with Dad if he wanted to take the helmet off. On the Fourth of July the pole was Uncle Sam, on Veterans' Day a soldier, on Halloween a ghost. The pole was Dad's only concession to glee. We were allowed a single Crayola from the box at a time. One Christmas Eve he shrieked at Kimmie for wasting an apple slice. He hovered over us as we poured ketchup saying: good enough good enough good enough. Birthday parties consisted of cupcakes, no ice cream. The first I brought a date over she said: what's with your dad and that pole? and I sat there blinking.

We left home, married, had children of our own, found the seeds of meanness blooming also within us. Dad began dressing the pole with more complexity and less discernible logic. He draped some kind of fur over it on Groundhog Day and lugged out a floodlight to ensure a shadow. When an earthquake struck Chile he laid the pole on its side and spray painted a rift in the earth. Mom died and he dressed the pole as Death and hung from the crossbar photos of Mom as a baby. We'd stop by and find odd talismans from his youth arranged around the base: army medals, theater tickets, old sweatshirts, tubes of Mom's makeup. One autumn he painted the pole bright yellow. He covered it with cotton swabs that winter for warmth and provided offspring by hammering in six crossed sticks around the yard. He ran lengths of string between the pole and the sticks, and taped to the string letters of apology, admissions of error, pleas for understanding, all written in a frantic hand on index cards. He painted a sign saying LOVE and hung it from the pole and another that said FORGIVE? and then he died in the hall with the radio on and we sold the house to a young couple who yanked out the pole and the sticks and left them by the road on garbage day.

Figure 2.2.

Activity—Club English:

The ultimate goal of this close-reading unit is to engrain in students

- the literary terminology they'll need to effectively discuss author's choices; and
- the connection between applying the term and discussing why it matters—the "So what" of it all.

When teaching a unit on literary terminology, there is the possibility that after two or so days of taking notes and writing down examples of terms and their definitions, your students are going to get antsy. When this happens, it's time to roll out the super-fun-they'll-never-see-it-coming Club English day!

This is a day when students practice applying terms to new, unfamiliar pieces of *music*. Use music instead of poetry or nonfiction because it's more accessible to all students in your room. Students who are struggling with the idea of mood can *hear* the mood in the singer's voice and in the melody paired with the diction. Students struggling with repetition and inference can *hear* how it matters in a piece of music.

All teenagers listen to music; not all teenagers appreciate poetry. By beginning the application of terms with an activity like this, students are more likely to understand and appreciate the significance of literary terms to the effectiveness of a piece. Additionally, if you later move on to a poetry unit, they will be able to see the connections between something they all love and have a relationship with (music) and something new and less familiar (poetry).

Choose a number of songs to play for your students. Print out the lyrics of each. Make copies for all your students. These should be songs that have lyrics that demonstrate examples of several of the literary terms you've been teaching. A list used in the past looks like this:

"Gloomy Sunday"—Billie Holiday
"Stay or Leave"—The Dave Matthews Band
"The Piano Has Been Drinking"—Tom Waits
"A Hymn to Him"—*My Fair Lady* soundtrack

Students should have their list of terms, definitions, and examples in front of them. Pass out highlighters, colored pencils, anything students want to use to create their "map" of annotations on the lyrics. Dictate a key if you think it would be more useful (i.e., pink highlighter on tone, yellow highlighter on imagery, etc.) but keep this simple—remember, the point is that students start to see and hear the terms in action in an accessible way.

"Gloomy Sunday"

Sunday is gloomy,
My hours are slumberless,
Dearest the shadows
I live with are numberless
Little white flowers will
never awaken you
Not where the black coach
of sorrow has taken you
Angels have no thought of
ever returning you
Would they be angry
if I thought of joining you
Gloomy Sunday.

Gloomy is sunday
with shadows I spend it all
My heart and I have
decided to end it all
Soon there'll be candles
and prayers that are sad,
I know, let them not weep,
let them know
that I'm glad to go

Death is no dream,
for in death I'm caressing you
With the last breath of my
soul I'll be blessing you

Gloomy Sunday
Dreaming
I was only dreaming
I wake and I find you
asleep in the deep of
my heart
dear

Darling I hope that my dream
never haunted you
My heart is telling you
how much I wanted you
Gloomy Sunday.

Figure 2.3.

Play each song and allow five to ten minutes for students to annotate the lyrics. Tell them to look for diction that could be multiple terms at once. For instance, "Gloomy" is an example of diction that connotes sadness and despair, which creates the mood of the song "Gloomy Sunday." Remember, we don't want them to only label terms—we want them to practice appreciating how each term can build on another to create more meaning. By the end of the annotation period, the text should be similar to that of figure 2.3.

After their five to ten minutes, facilitate a conversation about where they saw the terms applied. Don't settle for superficial answers. All statements should be followed with "this is important because . . ." Make them explain *why* the literary device they found affected the piece of music as a whole.

Assessment

After each of the songs has been played and annotated, have students choose one to compose a close-read paragraph about. This will force them to articulate

- where they see the terms being utilized;
- how they interact with each other; and
- whether or not these literary choices are effective for the audience.

These responses should give you, the teacher, a good idea of whether or not your class is adequately comfortable applying all the new academic language they've gathered, and how well they can articulate what they see as the effectiveness of those choices.

Taking It Further

For homework, assign a similar task. Have students come to school the next day with the printed lyrics of a song they are familiar with that they annotated for literary terms. Let them see how the things they love in their own life also utilize the very terms they've been studying in English class!

SUMMARY

This chapter demonstrates how to introduce, use, and build upon skills necessary for close reading. Close reading itself relies on critical thinking and original analysis on the part of the student and is therefore a pivotal part of the Common Core toolkit.

These exercises create an interactive relationship between the student and the text, thereby creating confidence in the student to navigate unfamiliar and intimidating texts with ease and skill. This skill is initially introduced here, but will be built upon in subsequent chapters.

Finally, the skill is practiced using quality literature, which is engaging to students of all abilities, with no superficial graphic organizers or worksheets. Students immediately begin interacting directly with the text, examining the "So what?" of authorial choices, thereby emulating a college-ready skill that will be necessary in Common Core assessments.

Chapter Three

The Great Gatsby

Applying the Skills of Close Reading

UNIT QUESTION: HOW DO YOU KNOW IF YOU'VE MADE IT?

INTRODUCTION

Teaching *The Great Gatsby* can be difficult. Modernism can be tough for students to dig into. And, inevitably, students just do not get why Gatsby, who is such an obvious dreamboat, would waste so much time and effort on the vacuous Daisy—it's a struggle to provide a logical and believable response. But what they *love* talking about is the novel's discussion of American social strata—something they all have some level of experience with.

This unit will discuss how to use Fitzgerald's classic *The Great Gatsby* as a vehicle for applying the skills of close reading. Additionally, this chapter will demonstrate how to include cross-curricular research and assessment possibilities into a unit without sacrificing classroom time devoted to the exploration of the novel.

COMMON CORE STANDARDS ADDRESSED

✍ **College and Career Readiness Anchor Standards for Reading**

2. Determine central ideas or themes of a text and analyze their development; summarize the key supporting details and ideas.

4. Interpret words and phrases as they are used in a text, including determining technical, connotative, and figurative meanings, and analyze how specific word choices shape meaning or tone.

6. Assess how point of view or purpose shapes the content and style of a text.

7. Integrate and evaluate content presented in diverse media and formats, including visually and quantitatively, as well as in words.

8. Delineate and evaluate the argument and specific claims in a text, including the validity of the reasoning as well as the relevance and sufficiency of the evidence.

9. Analyze how two or more texts address similar themes or topics in order to build knowledge or to compare the approaches the authors take.

10. Read and comprehend complex literary and informational texts independently and proficiently.

PRE-READING ACTIVITIES

Anticipatory Set

Consider who your students are before beginning this unit. Have they had access to comfortable homes their whole lives? Have their parents been able to send them to their school of choice rather than a neighborhood school? Generally speaking, are you talking to a room of Daisys and Toms, or Nicks, or Georges? This is important, because the unit should begin with a very simple question: Do you believe in the American Dream? Meaning, do you believe that if you work hard, you can have the life you want in this country?

Spend a little time letting the kids discuss and share out. You may have some cynics in the audience, but overwhelmingly students at the high school level believe the American Dream is true. Ask them where they got this perception. Did someone sit them down and tell them? Can they name shows or movies or other aspects of popular culture in which this has been the driving, essential concept?

Then steer the conversation toward the students' own lives—have they seen it work? Do they know people who have worked hard and attained "a way out" of their poverty? Do they know people who worked really hard, but it made no tangible difference to their quality of life?

Activity—Introducing the Evaluation of Sources

Often units on research and evaluation drag. It can seem to students like a series of tasks rather than an authentic learning experience, which may be why reteaching the skills is so often necessary.

Following the initial discussion above, instruct students to make a comprehensive list of their experiences that promote the idea of the American Dream. As a class, look over the list. How many of the sources are reality shows? Movies? Other scripted material?

Once students have made their list, instruct small groups to compose a one-to-two page reflection on the validity of these sources. When they evaluate the origin of the source, do they trust what the source has been telling them? Why or why not?

Activity—How Much Is Enough?

After evaluating these sources, ask your class how much money is "enough" money. Give students some whiteboard markers and have them put their numbers up on the board. The number should be an annual amount a person could count on—no lottery winning. The concept of the American Dream is often associated with success and comfort and security—how does that translate monetarily? What amount of money is "enough" for a person to say that they "made it"?

These answers could be a very intriguing place to start a research project or paper, or even a cross-curricular opportunity with math class: how much money can the average person in the nation/state/city expect to make . . .

- With a high school diploma?
- With a college degree?
- With a masters or PhD?

Cross-reference this with living expenses, interest rates, average debt. How much is enough? Think of the possibilities between informational and fictional texts, here. Exciting stuff!

Incorporating Nonfiction Texts

Though other disciplines will use almost exclusively nonfiction texts in their Common Core preparation, there are moments within a literature unit in which the incorporation of such texts can be extremely powerful, both for building the desired skill set and for understanding the importance of the fiction the students are studying.

In preparation for this unit, consider providing your students with TED Talks, articles, charts, and so on, that demonstrate the complexity of the issue of *access versus opportunity* in America.

Make sure students have something to *do* with these texts. For instance, students could:

- write a summary;
- find their own research that supports or negates the nonfiction's thesis;
- find an article that discusses these statistics within their community or a neighboring community;
- annotate the article for argument, purpose, and intended audience;
- write a summary of how the information presented aligns with their community.

Taking It Further

✍ Common Core College and Career Readiness Anchor Standards for Speaking and Listening

5. Make strategic use of digital media and visual displays of data to express information and enhance understanding of presentations.

This is also a good place to build in the technological standards that are built within Common Core. Students could create a multimedia presentation evaluating their research and summarizing their major findings. Really, the possibilities are endless.

What you may discover from this activity is a lot of disenchanted kids realizing they are already well along a predetermined path that they are going to need to fight to get off of. Because they live where they live and they have had what they have had, they are *statistically* already a Daisy, a Nick, a Gatsby, or a George, and that's the beginning of understanding Gatsby as a character and a text.

Activity—Reflecting on Firsthand Knowledge

Next, instruct students to brainstorm and compile a list of people for whom they have seen the American Dream work.

Then, have them list people for whom it did not work—people they know who worked hard, but it did not change their quality of life—people who continued to be a boat against the current, as Nick says all Americans are.

Conduct a class vote: after all of this anticipatory work, do they believe the dream is possible? Why or why not? Has anyone's view changed from day one? Why or why not? Keep a tally on the board for the entirety of the unit. Retake the vote intermittently throughout the unit—has anyone changed their mind?

Activity—Research Information and Evaluate Sources

✍ *11–12 RI1. Cite strong and thorough evidence to support analysis of what the text says explicitly as well as inferences drawn from the text, including determining where the text leaves matters uncertain.*

The next step is to create a list of questions that thematically tie in to *The Great Gatsby* but are also directly related to each of the students' lives. Have students pick one or two to research. They should return from this research with a multitude of sources that they have evaluated and found to be academic and trustworthy. Use this as an opportunity to teach or reteach MLA citations and analysis of reliable sources and as a connection between fiction and informative texts that is academic and authentic.

Here is a list of topics that could be used for this activity:

- The probability of individuals jumping financial strata from their parents' generation
- Access to higher education based on region
- Access to higher education based on parents' financial situation
- Access to internships, job opportunities, career building based on region and parents' financial situation
- Probability of *your* children being in the same economic stratum as you
- Probability that a magnet-school and/or private education will lead to access to higher education

These pre-reading activities and discussions will help students to better appreciate the novel and to recognize the novel's relevance to their own lives.

1920s Research

The following pre-reading project will turn students toward the specific content of the novel. An activity such as this would address the research anchor standards of the Common Core, specifically:

✍ **College and Career Readiness Anchor Standards for Writing 6–12**

7. Conduct short as well as more sustained research projects based on focused questions, demonstrating understanding of the subject under investigation.

Place students in small groups and assign them one of the following research topics:

- The Jazz Age
- The Roaring Twenties

- The Lost Generation
- Prohibition
- Modernism (in literature)
- F. Scott Fitzgerald

Students will conduct research on their topic and present the results of that research to their class.

Table 3.1 provides a rubric that can be used to score the presentations. What is notable about this rubric is that it requires students to cite their sources internally (for example, on individual presentation slides) as well as in a correctly formatted bibliography. The rubric also requires students to know and understand the information they are sharing, as opposed to simply reading slides or notecards.

CLOSE READING *THE GREAT GATSBY*

Gatsby is an excellent text to use paired with your close-reading unit. It will provide many opportunities to annotate and analyze passages. There is a purposefulness and preciseness to the *concrete details* in the novel, many of those details carrying a symbolic significance.

Colors

An example of significant detail is Fitzgerald's use of color in the text:

- Green: the color of money; one of the colors with which Daisy is always associated; the green light toward which Gatsby reaches out.
- White: Jordan and Daisy are constantly wearing white—this, the students may say, suggests purity. The point, though, is that it suggests a *projection* of purity, an illusion. It also associates Daisy with Godliness. She is dressed and described as a goddess—a deity—at least to Gatsby, and this confusion about the proper idols to worship is what leads to Gatsby's downfall. This color symbolism supports the theme that worshipping money (and she who represents money) is an American *sin*, one that is Gatsby's *hamartia,* or tragic flaw.
- Grey, as seen most prominently in the valley of ashes, but also peppered throughout the text, especially at Gatsby's parties. The valley of ashes that separates East and West Egg from the rest of New York is a symbol of the moral decay of the lost generation. Nick's initial description of the valley of ashes in chapter 2 is an excellent passage for practicing close reading.

Figure 3.1. Oral Presentation Rubric

20	*15*	*10*	*5*
Introduction			
The students have planned a clever and effective introduction.	The students have planned an effective introduction.	The students have planned an introduction, but it is not all that effective.	The students have not planned an introduction.
Body			
The body of the presentation contains detailed information that is relevant to the assignment and is clear to both the presenters and the audience.	The body of the presentation contains information that is relative to the assignment and clear to both the presenters and audience, but the information is vague.	The body of the presentation contains relevant information, but the information is confusing and is not clear to either the presenters or the audience or both.	The information in the body of the presentation is irrelevant to the assignment.
Delivery			
All presenters are clearly knowledgeable about the topic and are able to speak intelligently to the class about the topic, rather than just reading slides.	Some presenters are clearly knowledgeable about the topic and are able to speak intelligently to the class about the topic, rather than just reading slides.	One presenter is clearly knowledgeable about the topic and is able to speak intelligently to the class about the topic, rather than just reading slides.	No presenters are clearly knowledgeable about the topic and none are able to speak intelligently to the class about the topic, rather than just reading slides.
Sources			
Sources are clearly cited, with both internal citations and a formatted bibliography, and all information is correctly quoted or paraphrased.	Sources are correctly quoted or paraphrased, and a formatted bibliography is provided, but no internal citations are given.	Sources are quoted or paraphrased, but citations and/or bibliography is not correctly formatted.	Sources are not quoted or paraphrased and/or no citations or bibliography is given.
Conclusion			
The students have planned a clever and effective conclusion.	The students have planned an effective conclusion.	The students have planned a conclusion, but it is not all that effective.	The students have not planned a conclusion.

Repetition, motif, color symbolism, diction, connotation, and allusion are all explicitly present.

The Valley of Ashes, the land of "grey" is, besides an allusion to the River Styx, the place where morality becomes itself grey—love may exist between Myrtle and Tom, but it blooms in a land of decadence, decay, impropriety. Myrtle is, of course, killed here, with the murderer suffering no consequence.

By specifically comparing the paragraph that describes Tom Buchanan's home with the paragraph describing the valley of ashes, students will discover that there are patterns of diction and corresponding images that clearly connect the two, implying thereby that Tom Buchanan's home is also a symbol of moral decay.

Motifs

Repeating colors is one example of a motif, or pattern of images or symbols, in the novel. Fitzgerald embeds a number of these motifs into *The Great Gatsby*, the most notable being:

- time;
- celestial imagery (stars, moons, etc.);
- eyes;
- rising and falling.

Activity—Close Reading Chapter 1

The following reading guide will help students to recognize and appreciate the aforementioned motifs as they begin to read the novel. This guide will also prompt students to draw connections between their reading and the research they conducted.

Chapter 1 Reading Guide (Student Instructions) In your notebook, you will create a chart that looks roughly like table 3.2:

Table 3.2. Chapter 1

Quotation (pg.#)	*So What?*

As you read, use this chart to keep track of the following:

1. Colors. What colors are used to describe what (or whom)? Also, look for "color words" like bright, glistening, glowing, shining, and so on.
2. Time. Keep track of references to "time." The word *time* itself, but also words related to time.
3. Eyes. Keep track of descriptions of characters' eyes.
4. Celestial Imagery. This means references to the stars, the moon, the sun, the heavens, and so on.
5. Rising and Falling. There's a motif in this chapter of things rising and falling. Find examples of it.
6. Anything in the chapter that connects to these research topics:
   a. Jazz Age
   b. Lost Generation
   c. Roaring 20s
   d. Prohibition
   e. F. Scott Fitzgerald

Activity—Timed Writing

The following timed-writing assignment will require students to apply the work they did while reading chapter 1. Such an activity addresses the following Common Core standards:

✍ College and Career Readiness Anchor Standards for Writing 6–12

1. Write arguments to support claims in an analysis of substantive topics or texts, using valid reasoning and relevant and sufficient evidence.

4. Produce clear and coherent writing in which the development, organization, and style are appropriate to task, purpose, and audience.

Provide the following prompt to students as they enter the room:

Write 1 to 2 pages discussing Fitzgerald's use of colors and "color words" in Chapter 1 of The Great Gatsby*. Be sure to discuss the effect of those choices, and be sure to include specific examples from the text. Due at the end of the period.*

As always, it is important that students are not only *identifying* Fitzgerald's use of color, but also examining the *effect* of those details.

Activity—Passage Analysis in Chapter 1

Before moving on to chapter 2, guide students in closely analyzing a particular passage from chapter 1 (similar to what was done using the opening paragraph of Poe's "The Fall of the House of Usher" in the previous chapter).

An example of a suitable passage for this exercise is the final two paragraphs of chapter 1.

Get students started by instructing them to do the following:

Describe this passage using only one word. The word cannot appear in the passage. (*This will help students to identify the tone of the passage.*)

- Find the single most important piece of diction in the passage (only one word).
- Explain the significance of that piece of diction (use the words *diction*, *connote/connotes*, and *imply/implies*)
- Find all of the pieces of diction that have the same effect as the first piece.

Then, turn to imagery:

- Find the single most important image in the passage.
- Explain the significance of that image (use the words *imply/implies*).
- Find all of the images that have the same effect as the first piece.

As students are completing these tasks, they should be annotating, or marking their texts, as described in the previous chapter. The following are additional tips to aid students in effectively annotating their passage:

- Use one color highlighter to mark all *diction* that helps to create the tone/tones of your passage.
- Use another color highlighter to mark all *imagery* that helps to create the tone/tones of your passage.
- Draw lines (pen or pencil) connecting diction/imagery that creates a pattern. Remember: pattern = motif
- Fill the margins with notes.

At this point, students are prepared to complete the following task, which can be done individually or collaboratively, the end product being an organized commentary of the passage.

1. Compose 1 to 3 sentences describing . . .
   a.) the overall tone of the passage, or
   b.) two tones that exist simultaneously in the passage.
   The tone(s) should be words that do not appear in the passage.
2. Write a paragraph discussing the DICTION in the passage.
   - Identify patterns of diction.
   - Focus on how the diction creates the tone(s).

- Integrate Quotations!
- Use "connotation"/"connote."

3. Write a paragraph discussing the IMAGERY in the passage.
   - Identify patterns (and connections to the diction).
   - Focus on how the imagery creates the tone(s).
   - Integrate Quotations!
   - Use "imply"/"implies."
4. Make a connection between the tone(s) of this passage and the novel as a whole (this can be a connection to the plot, to the themes, to characterization, etc.).

Gatsby's Parties: Additional Close Reading Practice

Fitzgerald's descriptions of Gatsby's parties, which appear first in chapter 3 and then again in subsequent chapters, offer an additional opportunity for students to practice their close-reading skills.

Place students in groups, and assign each group a passage from the text describing Gatsby's party (almost any page from chapter 3 would work for this activity). Each group is responsible for creating all of the following:

Paragraph 1: Write one to three sentences describing specifically what is happening in the passage, and one to three sentences describing

a. the overall tone of the passage, or
b. two tones that exist simultaneously in the passage.

Paragraph 2: Discuss the DICTION in the passage.

a. Identify patterns of diction.
b. Focus on the diction's effect on the tone.
c. Integrate quotations!
d. Use the words "connotation"/"connote."

Paragraph 3: Discuss the IMAGERY in the passage.

a. Identify patterns (and connections to the diction).
b. Focus on the imagery's effect on the tone.
c. Integrate quotations!
d. Use the worlds: "imply"/"implies."

Paragraph 4: Make a connection between the tone of this passage and the novel as a whole (this can be a connection to the plot, to the themes, to characterization, etc.).

Close Reading Project and Exam

Once students have completed their reading of the novel, and have practiced their close reading skills along the way, they will participate in a final group project that will apply those skills and will culminate in a close-reading exam.

Provide two pivotal passages from *The Great Gatsby* to each group and give them the following handout. They will have to

- prepare a close read of the text with annotations, as well as
- prepare an oral presentation that discusses how the passages they were given develop the reader's understanding of the entire text.

This activity will address the following Common Core anchor standards:

✍ Common Core College and Career Readiness Anchor Standards for Speaking and Listening 6–12

4. Present information, findings, and supporting evidence such that listeners can follow the line of reasoning and the organization, development, and style are appropriate to task, purpose, and audience.

Gatsby *Close-Read Project (Student Instructions)*

Your group will present a commentary on your assigned passage (ten minutes minimum).

The presentation will consist of an in-depth, thoughtful, and thorough analysis of the passage. Look for the small, meticulous details that are significant (diction, imagery, motifs, etc.) and discuss the effect of those details on the bigger picture (the novel as a whole).

This is important. Your fellow classmates will be tested on these passages. It is your job to teach your passage effectively. Your peers are relying on you. The class is free to ask questions. That is not part of your ten minutes. I expect you all to hold one another accountable and to a high standard.

If you want to say something but can't answer the question, "So what?," don't say it.

Use the terms as much as possible. Make sure you use them appropriately and with a purpose (see the above statement regarding "So what?").

Organize your commentary *idea to idea*, not *top to bottom.*

Your passage should be displayed during the presentation (and annotated).

Close-Read Exam

Following the presentations, students will take a close-read exam in which they will be given a passage to annotate and write a commentary on. The students will not know which passage they will receive on the exam, but it will be a passage that was presented on previously. Students will not receive the passage that their group presented on.

This exam provides a rigorous formal assessment of the close-reading skills that the students have been practicing throughout the unit.

CHARACTERIZATION IN *THE GREAT GATSBY*

Besides being a text that allows multiple opportunities for students to hone their close-reading skills, *The Great Gatsby* is also filled with rich characters that warrant rigorous discussion in a classroom setting.

Who Is to Blame?

To begin with, *Gatsby* is a novel that ends in tragedy. Of the four principal characters, who is to blame for this tragedy? An argument could be made for Gatsby's blindness and obstinacy and relentless optimism, or Daisy's selfishness and self-preservation, or Nick's passivity, or Tom's ruthlessness, or the blame could fall on the concept of wealth in America itself.

This discussion requires students to have a full and nuanced understanding of each of these characters and also requires them to make an evaluation based upon that understanding. The discussion could culminate in an engaging classroom debate or an essay prompt. However, the larger point is, why does Fitzgerald leave it so ambiguous?

The Unreliable Narrator

This concept may dovetail nicely if the teacher is using this unit to teach or reteach the skill of evaluating sources of information. When teaching the different points of view from which a story can be told, consider the effect of a first-person perspective.

- What does Nick tell us?
- What can't he tell us?
- What does he choose not to tell us? (Track the drinking in the text—Nick says he's only been drunk a couple of times, and these times correspond to him being unable to provide the audience with a full account of things.)
- What is the effect of Fitzgerald's choice of point of view on our understanding of the novel?
- To what extent is this choice effective?

Students should be made aware that with any first-person narrator, a critical reader should question the reliability of that narrator.

Characters as Symbols of Social Status

Characters in *The Great Gatsby* serve as symbols of social status, and these class divisions are linked to the geography of the novel. The inhabitants of East Egg (Tom, Daisy) represent old, inherited, aristocratic money and status while the inhabitants of West Egg (Gatsby) represent new, entrepreneurial, pull-yourself-up-by-your-boot-straps money and status, with the valley of ashes (George, Myrtle) representing the lower class that is both ignored and exploited by the two Eggs.

An illustration of these class divisions can be found in chapter 2, at the party in Myrtle's apartment. In the chapter, Myrtle, Tom's mistress, is struck by Tom for repeatedly saying the name of Tom's wife, Daisy. Why can Tom hit Myrtle? We have no reason to believe he would ever hit Daisy.

Myrtle is from a different social class, and therefore can be treated harshly, whereas Daisy is from "old money" and would never be treated brutally by Tom. Tom later finds out that Daisy is having an affair with Gatsby and doesn't touch her. Myrtle attempts to speak to Tom as an equal, as well as to equate herself with Daisy, and in doing so she is attempting to act as a member of a social class that is above her own, and the result is a violent rejection.

Myrtle is an interesting character to examine in that her own failure foreshadows Gatsby's. Like Gatsby, she is desperately trying to be something that she is not—trying to rise in status, and like Gatsby, this endeavor fails violently.

FINAL ASSESSMENTS

By the end of the unit, students have studied the text in depth and have gained a masterful understanding of the implicit significance of concrete details, characterization, and symbolism, as well as the ability to research and connect outside information (nonfiction texts) to their study of literature.

The Great Gatsby Final Exam

What follows is a potential final unit exam. This exam can serve as a backwards map for the teacher.

Notice how Section 1 topics allow for nonfiction research crossover. Section 2 reviews themes and will demand quality understanding of the text as a whole. Section 3 forces students to look at patterns, motifs, and symbolism in the text and examine their purpose, and Section 4 asks for an understanding of character and character development.

Notice also that each section of the exam requires students to support their claims with specific details from the text.

✍ College and Career Readiness Anchor Standards for Writing 6–12

2. Write informative/explanatory texts to examine and convey complex ideas and information clearly and accurately through the effective selection, organization, and analysis of content.

9. Draw evidence from literary and/or informational texts to support analysis, reflection, and research.

Student Instructions

Section 1: Discuss how each of the following aspects of the 1920s life is reflected in the novel, *The Great Gatsby.* Each response should be 100–200 words in length and must include details from the text for support.

1. Lost Generation
2. Jazz Age
3. Prohibition

Section 2: Discuss how each of the following themes is developed in the novel, *The Great Gatsby*. Each response should be 100–200 words in length and should include details from the text for support.

1. False idols
2. Social Status
3. American Dream
4. Moral Decay

Section 3: Discuss the significance of each of the following motifs/symbols in the novel, *The Great Gatsby*. Each response should be 100–200 words in length and should include details from the text for support.

1. Color Patterns/Color Diction
2. Valley of Ashes
3. The Eyes of Dr. T. J. Eckleburg
4. Owl Eyes
5. Time

Section 4: Discuss how each of the following characters is developed in the novel, *The Great Gatsby*. Each response should be 100–200 words in length and should include details from the text for support.

1. Daisy
2. Tom
3. Nick
4. Gatsby
5. Jordan
6. Myrtle

Note: You will start to see overlap between topics, and that is okay. For example, a response to the topic of the Valley of Ashes certainly could (and probably should) include discussion of the Lost Generation and moral decay.

The Great Gatsby Short-Answer Exam

The following is another option for a summative exam on *The Great Gatsby*, this test requiring students to compose short-answer responses to three prompts chosen from a list of six. Notice again, that the exam requires students to include textual evidence to support their claims.

✍ College and Career Readiness Anchor Standards for Writing 6–12

10. Write routinely over extended time frames (time for research, reflection, and revision) and shorter time frames (a single sitting or a day or two) for a range of tasks, purposes, and audiences.

Student Instructions

Choose 3 of the following 6 to respond to. Reference specific examples from the text within your answer:

1. Describe Gatsby's relationship with Daisy.
2. Compare and contrast Gatsby and Tom.
3. What is Nick's role in *The Great Gatsby*? What does he add to the story, and how would the story have been different without him?
4. Who was responsible for Gatsby's death? Explain your choice.
5. How was Nick different from Daisy, Tom, and Jordan?
6. Suppose this novel had been written from Gatsby's point of view. How would the story have changed?

The Great Gatsby Final Essay

The following could be used as an in-class, timed writing assignment or as an opportunity for a full-process paper with multiple drafts.

✍ Common Core College and Career Readiness Anchor Standards for Writing

5. Develop and strengthen writing as needed by planning, revising, editing, rewriting, or trying a new approach.

Student Instructions

You will write a 3–6 page paper (750–1500 words) in response to one of the following:

1. What is Fitzgerald suggesting about the usefulness of being truthful?
2. Is Fitzgerald trying to show us an indifferent God that has abandoned society, or a caring God that society has abandoned?
3. What does this novel suggest about Fitzgerald's view of women?
4. What is the significance of the last paragraph of *The Great Gatsby*? Why does the text conclude the way it does?
5. How is this text a reflection of the struggle of the Lost Generation?
6. Discuss at least one (and no more than two) scene(s) that uses concrete details to convey significant meaning in the text.
7. How is color symbolism utilized in the text?
8. What connections do you see between the nonfiction articles we've read and *The Great Gatsby*? What is the significance of these connections?

Develop a thesis and support it with examples from the text.

SUMMARY

This chapter has demonstrated how to create a marriage between the natural incorporation of nonfiction texts and research as well as an in-depth study of the poetry of a text via close reading and literary analysis. The study of literature was never compromised or replaced, but rather repeatedly enhanced by outside research, evaluation, and analysis of nonfiction materials.

Notice how the impetus for all of the student assessments is always on the student. Teachers are not making long matching/multiple-choice/fill-in-the-blank tests. Students are always presented with rigorous assignments that insist on a masterful understanding of the text and of the skills they've been practicing. Students are writing, analyzing, drafting, revising, researching, and exploring the text, the skills, and secondary sources in order to craft their original thoughts. This is not only wonderful practice for the Common Core assessments, but is excellent for total college and career readiness.

Chapter Four

The Taming of the Shrew

An Introduction to Shakespeare

UNIT QUESTION: ARE YOU ACTING?

INTRODUCTION

This chapter presents a framework for using Shakespeare's *The Taming of the Shrew* to introduce students to Shakespeare and/or to introduce students to Shakespearean comedy. Strategies are presented for moving students past the difficulty of Shakespeare's language, which is the one factor that often leads students to dismiss the playwright, and to help them see just how relevant to their own social lives his plays can be. Also included in this chapter are specific lessons and discussion questions for each act, for key scenes and speeches, and for the analysis of filmed productions of the play.

Studying *Taming* will introduce students to key elements present in much of Shakespeare's work, such as . . .

- Disguise/Transformation;
- Play within a play;
- Thematic Allusions;
- Five-Act Structure; and
- Ambiguous language and stage direction and their effect.

The play will also introduce students to key elements of Shakespearean comedy, such as . . .

- strong women;
- bawdy humor; and
- comic characters.

This chapter will guide teachers in incorporating high-level critical thinking and high-level writing into the study of the play.

COMMON CORE STANDARDS ADDRESSED

✍ College and Career Readiness Anchor Standards for Reading 6–12

1. Read closely to determine what the text says explicitly and to make logical inferences from it; cite specific textual evidence when writing or speaking to support conclusions drawn from the text.

2. Determine central ideas or themes of a text and analyze their development; summarize the key supporting details and ideas.

3. Analyze how and why individuals, events, and ideas develop and interact over the course of a text.

5. Analyze the structure of texts, including how specific sentences, paragraphs, and larger portions of the text (e.g., a section, chapter, scene, or stanza) relate to each other and the whole.

7. Integrate and evaluate content presented in diverse media and formats, including visually and quantitatively, as well as in words.

> 8th Grade: Analyze the extent to which a filmed or live production of a story or drama stays faithful to or departs from the text or script, evaluating the choices made by the director or actors.
>
> 11th–12th Grade: Analyze multiple interpretations of a story, drama, or poem (e.g., recorded or live production of a play or recorded novel or poetry), evaluating how each version interprets the source text. (Include at least one play by Shakespeare and one play by an American dramatist.)

9. Analyze how two or more texts address similar themes or topics in order to build knowledge or to compare the approaches the authors take.

> 9th–10th Grade: Analyze how an author draws on and transforms source material in a specific work (e.g., how Shakespeare treats a theme or topic from Ovid or the Bible or how a later author draws on a play by Shakespeare).

10. Read and comprehend complex literary and informational texts independently and proficiently.

PRE-READING ACTIVITIES: A WAY IN

A great way to begin this unit is to view the first ten to fifteen minutes of a contemporary film, specifically 1999's *10 Things I Hate about You,* which is a "teen movie" adaptation of *The Taming of the Shrew*. The problem with teaching Shakespeare is that too often time, place, and language become barriers to student appreciation of what would otherwise be an engaging and relevant story.

Students cringe (and sometimes also moan or groan or roll their eyes) at the mere mention of Shakespeare. They see Shakespeare's work as something that is important to us—the adults—and that we are imposing that interest upon them. It is something to be tolerated, another inevitable high school hoop to jump through that bears no actual relevance to their lives.

This is especially true if the student has had a "bad" Shakespeare experience: a failed attempt at reading and understanding one of his plays. So don't start with Shakespeare. Don't even mention Shakespeare. Just show this movie, before even checking out the books. If you need to provide rationale (which you won't; they'll be happy enough to be watching a movie) tell them that the purpose is to review the previously studied elements of plot and conflict.

Tell the students that they will be watching the first ten to fifteen minutes of a film, and afterwards will be getting into groups to answer the following questions:

1. What is the setting?
2. Who are the characters?
3. What is the ground situation?
4. What is the inciting incident?
   (See chapter 6 for explanations of these two previous questions.)
5. What is the conflict?
6. Who is the protagonist?
7. Who/What is the antagonist?
8. Based on all of the above, what do you predict will happen in this story?

Remember not to mention Shakespeare (yet). We don't want their experience tainted. Show the movie up to the scene where Kat and Bianca's father declares that Bianca can date when Kat dates. At this point, a ground situation, inciting incident, conflict, protagonist, and antagonist have been established. Basically, Bianca is the nice sister that every guy wants to date; Kat is the abrasive sister that every guy is afraid of; their father is overly protective and won't allow either to date, until he decides that he will allow Bianca (who desperately wants to date) to begin dating when Kat (who has no interest in dating) begins dating.

Group responses to the questions above will vary based on which character they believe is the protagonist (Kat, Bianca, or Joey, or a combination), and these differences will drive the whole-class discussion that follows. Groups will also come up with wild and variant predictions of where the story will go next.

Activity—Gender Expectations

In the clip, Kat is referred to (by a school official) as a "heinous bitch." In the subsequent lesson, lead a conversation about the use of the word "bitch" and its connotations. If time allows, students may conduct research on the word's origins and evolution.

Drive the discussion toward an awareness of gender expectations and their relationship to words like "bitch." What is expected of a woman (by society, by men, by other women), and what are the consequences of failing to meet those expectations? Likewise, what is expected of a man, and what are the consequences of failing to meet those expectations? The students may note that "bitch" can be used to refer to either a man or a woman, but when referring to a woman, the word implies masculinity while implying femininity when used to refer to a man. In either case, the word is a result of failure to meet established expectations.

As you prepare to read act 1 with your class, inform the students that in 1590, when the play was believed to have been written, the word *bitch* was not used in the way that we use it today and in the way that we discussed earlier, but that a synonym for that earlier use of the word *bitch* is *shrew*. *Shrew*, as it used in the play, carries similar connotations to the word *bitch* as it was used to describe Kat in *10 Things I Hate about You*. With this in mind, students can make predictions about the content of the play based upon its title.

Addressing the Problem of Language

At this point, it would be fine to check out the books and begin dealing with the play itself. Some students, once they have a copy in hand, will notice Katherine and Bianca in the list of characters; others won't realize the connection to the film until the class begins reading act 1.

It is important, though, to address the barriers that stand in the way of student appreciation of Shakespeare's plays, particularly the barrier of language. If you ask a group of students *why* they struggle with Shakespeare's language, you will often get the response that it is written in Old English. This is the first misconception we can dispel.

Old English was used roughly until the Norman Invasion of the eleventh century. *Middle English* was used roughly until the Great Vowel Shift in the fifteenth century, which means that Shakespeare wrote in *Modern* English, not Old English.

To demonstrate the stark difference between Old English and Shakespeare, show students an excerpt of Old English, such as the one below from the opening of *Beowulf*, and ask them to summarize the stanza with their partner:

> Hwæt! We Gardena in geardagum,
> þeodcyninga, þrym gefrunon,
> hu ða æþelingas ellen fremedon.
> Oft Scyld Scefing sceaþena þreatum,

The response from students will probably be that they can't summarize any of this because it's not in English. Then ask them to try the following, which is an example of Middle English from Chaucer's *Canterbury Tales*:

> Whan that aprill with his shoures soote
> The droghte of march hath perced to the roote,
> And bathed every veyne in swich licour
> Of which vertu engendred is the flour;

Students should be able to recognize many more of the words in this excerpt, but should still struggle to make meaning. Then show them Shakespeare:

> To be, or not to be: that is the question:
> Whether 'tis nobler in the mind to suffer
> The slings and arrows of outrageous fortune,
> Or to take arms against a sea of troubles,
> And by opposing end them?

What students should recognize is that despite the difficulties they may have with Shakespeare, it is actually much closer to *their* English than they may have thought, especially when compared to Old or Middle English.

In fact, the only word from the Shakespeare passage that most students are unfamiliar with is *'tis*, which brings us to the next step in breaking down the language barriers between Shakespeare and students. By understanding the following features of Shakespeare's English, students will have an increased chance of understanding his plays.

1. Contractions. The contractions students find in Shakespeare's plays are different from the contractions we use today (don't, can't, won't, etc.). These unfamiliar contractions often stop readers in their tracks. The most frequent

of these contractions is the aforementioned 'tis. When informed that in such contractions the apostrophe represents a missing letter (as it does in don't, can't, won't, etc.), students will probably be able to determine that *'tis* is a contraction of *it is*, and will also be able to recognize the past tense version, *'twas*, as *it was*.

Another common example is a single-word contraction in which a letter (and thereby a syllable) is replaced by an apostrophe, such as in the contraction of *ever* to *e'er*. The reason for the contraction, in context, is probably to eliminate a syllable for the purposes of meter.

Students hesitate because they do not know how to read *e'er*—they usually assume that the apostrophe indicates a stop and that the sound on each side of it should be pronounced separately—and they fail to recognize that it is a familiar word, not a foreign one. Students should be instructed to read such contractions *without* stopping—to roll right through them—and the contracted word will sound like the familiar word.

2. Pronouns. A common problem for students is all of those second-person pronouns, such as *thou* and *thee.* Students should know, when they see them, that they mean *you*.

3. Syntax. Shakespeare often played around with the syntax of his sentences, probably for purposes of meter. An example is the following phrase from *Taming*: "Schoolmasters will I keep." Students should recognize that, in this case, Shakespeare has placed the auxiliary verb before the subject, and placed the object before them both. In standard syntax, the phrase would read like this: "I will keep schoolmasters."

Are You Acting?

Once students have been given strategies to tackle Shakespeare's language, the next step is to introduce the guiding question for this unit of study, which is "Are you acting?" Approach this question by first asking the students how often, in their lives, they are *performing*, or playing a role or part, that is not entirely their true self. Initially, some students will declare that they never perform and that they are always their true self, which is in itself a performance, and if you press a bit upon this claim, most students will come to the realization that we *all* perform, and we each may play multiple roles, depending on the situation. Ask students *why* they are performing, *for whom* are they performing.

The relevance of this discussion will become apparent to students early on in the reading of the play itself, which begins not with act 1 but with the *Induction.*

APPROACHES TO THE INDUCTION

The Induction to *The Taming of the Shrew* is important to discuss because it establishes themes that are present throughout the rest of the play. However, the Induction is rarely included in stage or film versions of the play, in part because it is seemingly incomplete. Basically, the Induction serves as a narrative frame for the play, which ends with a character (Christopher Sly) watching a performance of *The Taming of the Shrew*. However, the frame is "broken" and is not completed at the end of the play.

An instructor has two options for dealing with the Induction: to assign students to read the Induction (preferably in small groups or as a class), or to paraphrase the events of the Induction and discuss how those events establish central themes. The latter option allows for a quicker entry into the play itself and thereby earlier connections to the film, the discussion of gender expectations, and the discussion of performance.

A paraphrase of the Induction would go something like this: Christopher Sly, a drunken beggar, is kicked out of a bar and passes out. A lord comes along with his entourage and decides to take the passed-out Sly home and play a trick on him. Sly is cleaned up and placed in the lord's bed, and when he wakes up, the lord (now dressed as a servant) and his attendants make Sly believe that *he* is a lord, and has been all along—his life as a drunken beggar was a bad dream. Sly is skeptical at first, but doesn't take long to buy into what he is being told. A page is then dressed up as a lady and presented to Sly as his wife. Then a group of traveling actors is hired to perform a play for Sly. The play is *The Taming of the Shrew*. Begin act 1.

What is important here is that the Induction establishes the theme of *deception*, evident in the trick played on Sly. With our unit question in mind (Are you acting?), it should be brought to the attention of the students that, technically, *deception* is a synonym for *acting*, and students will find, as the play progresses, that deception and performance are closely related.

Another theme established in the Induction is *transformation*—suggested by the transformations undergone by Sly, the lord, and the page—and the related motif of *disguise*, a ubiquitous element to *The Taming of the Shrew* and to Shakespearean comedy in general.

Furthermore, the Induction manufactures the situation of a "play within a play," a device found in several of Shakespeare's plays, including *Hamlet*, *Henry IV Part One*, and *A Midsummer Night's Dream*. Essentially, what an audience is watching when they watch *The Taming of the Shrew* (with the Induction included) is technically not *The Taming of the Shrew,* but Christopher Sly watching *The Taming of the Shrew*. Let's say that again: We are watching Christopher Sly watch *The Taming of the Shrew*. We are watching a play within a play.

Discuss with students the *effect* of that choice. What is the effect of a "play within a play?" Ultimately, the goal is to drive the students toward appreciating that a play within a play reminds the audience that what they are seeing on stage is a performance—the characters on stage are *actors* playing a *part*. It is all deception. This observation will become more poignant as students read further into the play and discover characters who, like all of us, are performing.

✍ Common Core Anchor Standard for Reading number 2 requires students to "determine central ideas or themes of a text and analyze their development." The recognition of key themes established in the Induction is the first step in that process.

READING THE PLAY

There are several different ways to read a Shakespeare play—whole class, small groups, pairs, individually—and it is advisable to use a combination of all these strategies. It is also advisable to read the first scene of act 1 together as a class.

But here's the problem with the first scene of Shakespeare plays: they usually consist of two people walking out on stage and talking blah, blah, blah about who-knows-what. It can be very easy, in these opening scenes, to lose the students.

Activity—Active Reading (Literally)

One strategy to combat this is to make the reading of the first scene a bit more visual. Add some movement.

- Assign students (or ask for volunteers) for each role.
- Place the readers along the peripheries of an open area of the classroom. The rest of the class has their books out and are following along.
- Have characters enter and exit as instructed by the text.
- When it is a student's turn to read, the rule is that they must be *moving* while they are reading.

The effect of this strategy is that it provides a visual element: something for the struggling readers to latch onto. The teacher is right there in the middle of the action, reading stage directions and "pausing" the scene for clarification, commentary, or discussion.

Guiding Questions for Act 1

It is also helpful, when approaching a scene, to provide students with a focusing question—something that, in the end, all students can walk away with an understanding of, regardless of whatever else is or is not understood. An example of such a focusing question for act 1, scene 1 of *The Taming of the Shrew* is the following:

> How are male expectations for a woman (and a wife) revealed in this scene, particularly by the males' descriptions of Katherine and Bianca?

As the class progresses through the scene, point out male descriptions of Katherine, male descriptions of Bianca, and the implied reasons for these descriptions. Students will recognize that Katherine is repeatedly referred to as devilish, while Bianca is repeatedly referred to as mild, and that these descriptions are directly connected not to their physical appearance but to their attitude and demeanor, particularly the extent to which they are either quiet or outspoken, revealing that what the men in this play desire is a mild, quiet woman who would potentially make an obedient wife.

Scene 2 of act 1 can be approached in a similar manner, and a suitable question to focus the reading is the following:

> What inferences can we make about the character of Petruchio? List (and use sticky notes to identify) specific lines of dialogue that help us to make these inferences.

Students will probably observe that Petruchio is bold and confident and maybe even loud. They may even claim that he is a potential match (in two senses of the word) for Katherine. These are all valid inferences, but the vital element is to push students to provide specific references to the text that support these inferences.

Guiding Questions for Additional Acts

What follows are examples of questions that can be used to focus students' reading of act 2. Act 2 consists of one long scene, and therefore can be split into several smaller parts, each with its own focusing question:

- What are some possible explanations for Katherine's behavior?
- Based upon their first meeting, what predictions would you make about Katherine and Petruchio's future relationship?
- How is Baptista's character developed in this act?

Besides focusing the students' reading of the text, questions such as these can be used later as assessment items, either as essay or short-answer questions. It is important to remember, both during discussions and on written assessments, to *require students to provide specific textual evidence* for their responses, a skill that is vital to the practice of critical reading and to meeting the Common Core Standards for Reading.

Here are additional questions that can be used while reading the play and for later assessment of students' understanding and appreciation of the play.

Act 3, scene 1: How does Bianca in this scene compare or contrast with Bianca in other scenes? What themes are reflected by Bianca's behavior in this scene?

Act 3, scene 2: How would you explain Petruchio's behavior before, during, and after the wedding? What is he trying to accomplish?

Act 4: To what extent do the events of act 4 constitute domestic violence? (This act may be enhanced by a discussion of domestic violence, or student research on the topic, particularly types of domestic violence—physical, emotional, economic, etc.)

Act 5: Who is the "real" Bianca? What do her words and actions in act 5 reveal about her character?

End of play: Has Kate been tamed?

USING FILM TO ENHANCE THE READING OF THE PLAY

Shakespeare's plays were not written for students to read and analyze; rather, they were written for audiences to watch and enjoy, and watching a production of a Shakespeare play can be a valuable experience for a student, both as a source of enjoyment and as a basis for analysis.

Most teachers can probably remember, from their high school days, reading the book and then watching the movie. But this approach is not the only option. A filmed production of a work of literature can be integrated into and used in tandem with the reading of the work it is adapting, and an appreciation of the choices being made in the adaptation is a requirement of the Common Core.

✍ *8RL7: Analyze the extent to which a filmed or live production of a story or drama stays faithful to or departs from the text or script, evaluating the choices made by the director or actors.*

11–12RL7: Analyze multiple interpretations of a story, drama, or poem (e.g., recorded or live production of a play or recorded novel or poetry), evaluating how each version interprets the source text. (Include at least one play by Shakespeare and one play by an American dramatist.)

Shakespeare's plays include very little stage direction—mostly just *Enters* and *Exits*. From the perspective of a director or an actor or even a reader, there is a great deal that is left open to interpretation.

An example of this comes in act 2 of *The Taming of the Shrew*. Toward the end of the scene (act 2 is all one scene), Petruchio and Katherine face Baptista (Katherine's father) and the other suitors after their highly contentious (and rather crude) first meeting. Petruchio declares to Baptista that he and Katherine will be married on Sunday. Katherine, in keeping with her character, responds, "I'll see thee hanged on Sunday first!"

Petruchio proceeds to declare that he and Katherine had fallen madly in love, that she had been unable to stop kissing and hugging him, and that he and she had decided that "in company" she would still act like a shrew, while acting lovingly in private. And what does Katherine, who has matched Petruchio line for line the entire scene, have to say about this? Nothing. She is silent. There is no stage direction indicating that she has exited or anything else that would explain her sudden silence.

Students offer possible suggestions—she has given up, she actually loves him, she is biding her time—but the fact is that Shakespeare's text leaves the matter ambiguous. It is open to the interpretation of an actor and director. In Franco Zeffirelli's 1967 film version of *Taming*, the director makes a clear choice, or series of choices, that presents a complex solution to the ambiguity. While making his claims regarding their relationship, Petruchio is twisting Katherine's arm behind her back. It is clear that, if she could, she would be protesting vociferously, but she is instead silent.

Petruchio eventually shoves Katherine into a locked room, which explains her silence for the remainder of the scene. This is when the performance gains complexity; though Katherine's frustration and ire for Petruchio are abundantly clear, the scene ends with a look that implies intrigue and longing for Petruchio.

Another scene that benefits from the examination of a production—and the choices made in that production—is act 3, scene 1, in which each of Bianca's two disguised suitors reveals their identity to her. It is implicit in Shakespeare's text that Bianca is not necessarily the meek, mild maiden that she appears to be, and in the 1980 BBC Television production of *The Taming of the Shrew*, this implied duplicity in Bianca is made explicit by the choice to make the scene sexually suggestive.

Regardless of the scene, or even the play, it is useful to ask students to analyze the choices being made in a staged or filmed adaptation. Student discussion of the director's interpretation of Shakespeare's text—including the extent to which they agree or disagree with the interpretation—is an exercise that will aid in the development of critical readers and thinkers.

✍ In addition, it is a requirement of the Common Core that students in the upper grade levels are able to draw inferences when there are ambiguities in a text.

11–12RL1. Cite strong and thorough textual evidence to support analysis of what the text says explicitly as well as inferences drawn from the text, including determining where the text leaves matters uncertain.

SHAKESPEAREAN CONVENTIONS

As stated in the introduction to this chapter, *The Taming of the Shrew* has many ingredients that make it a good introduction to Shakespeare's plays. For any play that is being taught as the students' first Shakespeare experience (probably in the eighth or or ninth grade), at least one goal of the unit should be to familiarize students with common elements of Shakespeare's plays that they are likely to reencounter in future courses. The following is a list of such elements that can be introduced while reading and studying *The Taming of the Shrew*.

Allusions

In his plays, Shakespeare often reinforces themes or motifs through meaningful allusions. First of all, students should be aware that an allusion is a reference to something well-known from history, mythology, the Bible, art, popular culture, or other literature.

Shakespeare places several such allusions in *The Taming of the Shrew,* frontloading several of them into the Induction and act 1. For example, in scene 2 of the Induction, reference is made to a series of paintings depicting scenes from Ovid's *Metamorphoses*. First of all, the title of Ovid's poem itself presents a clear connection to the theme of transformation, and all of the scenes depicted involve a transformation or disguise of some sort, so that the effect of the allusion is to aid in establishing a central theme (and motif) of the play.

Students may also observe that each of the depicted scenes in this allusion to *Metamorphoses* involves male dominance over a woman, foreshadowing an inescapable aspect of the play.

✍ It is worth noting here that Shakespeare's treatment of a theme from Ovid is specifically cited in the College and Career Readiness Anchor Standards for 9th to 10th Grade Reading.

9–10RL9: Analyze how an author draws on and transforms source material in a specific work (e.g., how Shakespeare treats a theme or topic from Ovid or the Bible or how a later author draws on a play by Shakespeare).

Five-Act Structure

Students should also be made aware that all of Shakespeare's plays are made up of five acts and that these acts correspond (sometimes loosely, sometimes tightly) to the elements of the plot triangle (or plot curve). In general, act 1 of a Shakespeare play is the exposition, in which the setting, characters, and conflict are introduced, followed by the rising action in act 2, which may spill into act 3.

While the actual *climax* of any Shakespeare play is up for debate, a key or climactic scene often occurs near the end of act 3 or in act 4, with the resolution coming in act 5. Students can "map" this 5-act plot structure onto any Shakespeare play, *The Taming of the Shrew* included.

Comic Characters

Shakespeare's plays are filled with comic characters, and this does not apply only to the comedies. In Shakespearean tragedies, such characters provide comic relief. In a comedy, there is less need for relief, but comic characters (such as Grumio and Biondello in *The Taming of the Shrew*) provide much of the slapstick or "low" comedy (see "Bawdy Humor" below).

Throughout the plays, these comic characters have some common characteristics. For one, they are often servants of some kind. Also, they often utilize puns (students should definitely leave a Shakespeare play familiar with what a pun is), such as in the beginning of act 1, scene 2, when Grumio (Petruchio's servant) confuses Petruchio's command to knock on the door with a command to strike his master.

Role Reversal

Speaking of servants, it is not uncommon in Shakespeare's plays to see the type of role reversal that we see between Lucentio and Tranio in *The Taming of the Shrew*, particularly a role reversal between a master and his subordinate.

It is also not uncommon, as in the case of Tranio, for a subordinate in Shakespeare's plays to surpass his or her master in intelligence and cunning. Tranio comes up with all of the angles and particulars in Lucentio's plan to woo Bianca, and he presents a stark contrast to Lucentio's other servant, who, as a comic character, is a blithering idiot.

Bawdy Humor

Bawdy humor is, quite simply, vulgar or obscene humor. This type of humor is common in Shakespeare's comedies, but like comic characters, it can also be found in the tragedies and histories, the most notable being the famous Sir John Falstaff of *Henry IV* Parts I and II and *The Merry Wives of Windsor*.

This type of humor is often driven by puns—in this case "dirty" puns. A prime example of such humor in *The Taming of the Shrew* is the initial meeting between Katherine and Petruchio, in the middle of act 2, scene 1. The scene is peppered with puns that, upon examination, are likely to make both you and your students blush.

Strong Women

When it comes to wit and depth of character, the men in *The Taming of the Shrew*, excluding Petruchio, are no match for either Katherine or Bianca. Particularly in the comedies, Shakespeare's women are often the strongest and sharpest characters in the play.

It is worth mentioning that Shakespeare's women can only be liberated and witty in the comedies, never the straight plays. Shakespeare writes many extraordinary women, many of whom use disguise or performance to free themselves from the restrictions of their gender (for example, Rosalind, Portia, Viola). Indeed, this is a trope in Shakespearean comedies—the women who, once disguised or "performing" can truly be their authentic, clever selves.

ASSESSMENTS

Short-Answer Exams (acts 1 and 2)

The two short-answer exams that follow can be given following the reading of acts 1 and 2, respectively. Each exam meets the following Common Core Standards.

✍ College and Career Readiness Anchor Standards for Reading 6–12

1. Read closely to determine what the text says explicitly and to make logical inferences from it; cite specific textual evidence when writing or speaking to support conclusions drawn from the text.

2. Determine central ideas or themes of a text and analyze their development; summarize the key supporting details and ideas.

3. Analyze how and why individuals, events, and ideas develop and interact over the course of a text.

5. Analyze the structure of texts, including how specific sentences, paragraphs, and larger portions of the text (e.g., a section, chapter, scene, or stanza) relate to each other and the whole.

Induction and Act 1 Short-Answer Test (with instructor notes)

Instructions: Write a one-to-two paragraph short-answer response to each of the following.

1. Discuss the role of the Induction. Be specific, but you can paraphrase. 10 pts.

A good answer discusses the fact that the Induction establishes the themes of transformation/disguise, deception/performance, and role reversal and explains how the Induction establishes those themes. A full 10-point answer will also discuss that the Induction establishes a play within a play, which constantly reminds the audience that everything they are seeing is a performance.

2. Discuss the role of act 1 in a 5-act structure, using act 1 of *The Taming of the Shrew* as an example. Include at least 3 specific references to the text. 10 pts.

A good answer will explain that the role of act 1 in a 5-act structure is exposition and will also explain that exposition introduces things like setting, characters, conflict, theme, etc. A full 10 will go on to identify the setting (Padua), the characters (especially protagonist(s), antagonist(s), etc.), conflict, and theme.

3. Discuss how expectations for a woman (and a wife) are revealed in this scene. Include at least 3 specific references to the text. 10 pts.

The main thing here is specific evidence. Most students will answer that the scene demonstrates that a woman (and wife) is expected to be quiet and gentle (like Bianca) and because Katherine is not quiet and gentle, she is deemed a shrew. But to get a full 10, the student needs to give at least 3 specific examples from the play that show this. An answer without 3 or more examples can't get more than a 6.

4. Discuss the effects of Shakespeare's allusions in both the Induction and act 1. Include at least 3 specific references to the text. 10 pts.

First of all, the answer should show that the student knows what an allusion is. The student needs to refer to at least three specific allusions. In class, we discussed three from the Induction and one from act 1, scene 1 (but there are others). That much gets a 7. For a full 10, the student needs to explain the effect of the allusions (most students will say that the allusions reinforce the theme of transformation/disguise and foreshadow male dominance over a woman).

5. Discuss the character of Petruchio. What inferences can we make about him based on act 1, scene 2? Include at least 3 specific references to the text. 10 pts.

Most students will probably say that Petruchio is bold and confident (maybe even a male version of Katherine). Whatever the student's claim is, the main thing is that the student gives at least 3 specific examples for support. An answer without 3 or more examples from the text cannot get more than a 6.

Act 2 Short-Answer Test (with instructor notes)

Instructions: Write a one to two paragraph short answer response to each of the following.

1. What are some possible reasons for Katherine's shrewish behavior? Be sure to provide specific examples from act 2 for support.

Most responses will be along the lines of "Katherine is jealous of Bianca." A full-credit answer should give good, specific support for this from the play, such as anything demonstrating that Bianca is favored over Katherine, particularly by their father.

2. Describe Petruchio and Katherine's first meeting. Be sure to include discussion of bawdy humor. Based on this scene, what predictions would you make about their future relationship? Be sure to provide specific examples from act 2 for support. Feel free to also discuss examples from Zeffirelli's film version.

Bawdy humor is rude, vile, offensive humor, which is common in Shakespeare's comedies but is seen in the tragedies and histories, as well. Basically, they are dirty jokes, usually involving puns. So the scene is basically Petruchio and Katherine volleying witty, sexually charged insults at one another. Petruchio would probably say that it went well; Katherine would probably say that she hates him, but actually she's falling in love with him. I think what we, as an audience, see is that they are perfect for one another.

The predictions can be pretty much anything that is plausible and implied by the text (or film).

Again, a full-credit answer should include good, specific support.

3. From line 320 on, Katherine stops protesting (and speaking altogether), even after Petruchio's lies in his speech. How do you explain this, given how vocal she has been up to this point? Why does she suddenly go silent? Be sure to provide specific examples from act 2 for support. Feel free to also discuss examples from Zeffirelli's film version.

Most students will probably say that Katherine stops protesting because she's really in love with Petruchio, which is what the film suggests. The film also shows Petruchio physically restraining her. What I'm looking for is any answer that makes sense and can be supported. Again, a full-credit answer should include specific support, either from the film or the text (or both).

4. How is Baptista's character developed in this act? Be specific, and support your answer with details from the play.

There is substantial support in this act that shows Baptista to be a less-than-great father. He both puts Bianca ahead of Katherine and puts money ahead of both of them. What is required is specific support from the play that demonstrates this.

The Taming of the Shrew Final Essay

The following essay assignment should be given after students have finished reading and discussing the play, and can take the form of either an on-demand, timed essay or a full-process, multi-draft essay. The assignment meets the following Common Core Standards.

✍ College and Career Readiness Anchor Standards for Reading 6–12

1. Read closely to determine what the text says explicitly and to make logical inferences from it; cite specific textual evidence when writing or speaking to support conclusions drawn from the text.

2. Determine central ideas or themes of a text and analyze their development; summarize the key supporting details and ideas.

3. Analyze how and why individuals, events, and ideas develop and interact over the course of a text.

✍ College and Career Readiness Anchor Standards for Writing 6–12

1. Write arguments to support claims in an analysis of substantive topics or texts, using valid reasoning and relevant and sufficient evidence.

8. Draw evidence from literary and/or informational texts to support analysis, reflection, and research.

The Taming of the Shrew Final Essay (student instructions)

Choose one of the following questions and compose a 1,000- to 1,500-word essay in response:

1. Has Katherine been tamed?
2. How have Katherine and Bianca's roles reversed by the end of the play?

Possible Sources:

The Taming of the Shrew by William Shakespeare

The Taming of the Shrew 1967 film version directed by Franco Zeffirelli

The Taming of the Shrew 1980 TV version, British Broadcasting Corporation

"*The Taming of the Shrew*: This Is Not a Woman Being Crushed" by Maddy Costa, *The Guardian,* January 17, 2012

The following are sample student responses to each of the two prompts. Both samples were written by tenth-grade students.

Student Sample 1

An Exercise in Misogyny

Taming of the Shrew *by William Shakespeare tells the tale of a shrew, Kate, having to marry before her mild maid of a sister, Bianca, may marry. This results in Katherine being married off to an abusive man named Petruchio, who wears her down mentally and physically until she is forced to give in to his demands. Katherine's shrewish attitude was not "tamed," it was forced out of her in the presence of Petruchio.*

From the beginning, Petruchio did not have the approval of Katherine as a husband. Their very first meeting is a conversation in which Katherine acts very cold towards him and even hits him. Katherine continues the conversation to make threats that should make him leave, but he only takes this as an invitation to make sexual advances. Petruchio takes Katherine's threatening words to suggest that he will have, [his] tongue in [her] tail. By speaking like this in their first meeting, it shows Petruchio's ideas of what women should be and his lack of consideration for how she feels. Katherine would have rather seen him dead than marry him, but Petruchio decided for their wedding to be that Sunday. He showed up late and then he rushed Katherine away from her family only to let her fall into mud and then deny her food. It reaches the point where Katherine is, "starved for meat [and] giddy for lack of sleep." This was Petruchio's plan to "tame" her. He deprived her of the necessities of life and Katherine believed that her only way to be fed or allowed to sleep was to not agitate Petruchio. He physically and psychologically abused her until she put the blame on herself for why he was in a bad mood. When Petruchio and Katherine return for Bianca and Lucentio's wedding, Katherine does all she can to stay there. Petruchio demands a kiss from Katherine and she refuses until he says that they should go home. Katherine did not want to kiss him, but saw it as the only way to stay in her home and not leave with Petruchio. Petruchio continuously abused her to the point where Katherine was fearful to question him. This abuse should not be mistaken as a change of attitude for Katherine.

Although Katherine only changed her ways because of the abuse she was going through, she had acts of defiance that showed her attitude was still there. When Katherine was trying on clothes for her sister's wedding, she found a hat that she liked. Petruchio thought it to be ugly and not big enough to meet his standards. Katherine demanded that, "[her] tongue will tell the anger of [her] heart." Katherine began to speak how she did before she was married to Petruchio, showing that her mentality and attitude had not changed. She argued until Petruchio had an outburst and started to yell at the tailor. Katherine did speak her mind, but stopped because she began to fear Petruchio. While at Petruchio's house, he claimed that time would be whatever time he said it was after Katherine had argued with him. Later, as they are approaching Katherine's home, Petruchio makes a comment about the moon, and Katherine persists that it is the sun shining. Petruchio tells her that, "it shall be moon . . . or e'er I journey to your father's house." Katherine knew that this was her only opportunity to return home, so she gives up the argument. Katherine only stopped talking when Petruchio threatened to not let her see her family. That is not a woman "tamed," it is a woman fearful that she will not see her family unless she submits to what Petruchio says. As the men are eating, Petruchio sends her to fetch Bianca and Hortensio's widow. In the film adaptation by Franco Zeffirelli, Katherine returns holding each woman by the ear. This act of cruelty is similar to Katherine tying her sister to a chair earlier in the play, before she met Petruchio. Calm and even tempered woman to not go get people by the ear. Katherine retained her attitude through her cruel actions until the very end. This shows that she still had the capacity to be violent and "shrewish."

Taming of the Shrew *is a wonderful example of, "an exercise in misogyny," as Maddy Costa of* The Guardian *states. It shows that woman are to be manipulated and beat down until they comply to the will of the man. This happened to Katherine through lack of food and sleep combined with threats to not let her see her family. Even though she went through this abuse, Katherine shows that she has not been "tamed" and is only acting out of fear.*

Student Sample 2

The Resilience of Katherine and Bianca

In The Taming of the Shrew, *Shakespeare showcases a duality between sisters, exemplifying an undesirable shrew as the elder and a well behaved maiden as the younger. The polarity between the two is immediately apparent with one the sisters representing the "ideal woman" and the other as completely repelling. Throughout the play, Bianca (the maiden) and Katherine (the shrew) are consistently portrayed in this way until the very end. This is when the sister's roles seem to reverse entirely—with Bianca disobeying her husband and Katherine lecturing her on her unsatisfactory ways. Despite this, there is not enough evidence to show that Katherine and Bianca have truly switched sides. Conversely, one might say something else entirely—that Bianca and Katherine haven't really changed at all.*

Firstly, Bianca's personality can easily be interpreted alternately to the perfect quiet maiden. Because Shakespeare only wrote the most necessary stage directions, Bianca's role can be perceived in a multitude of ways. For instance, in Franco Zeffirelli's 1967 adaptation of The Taming of the Shrew, *the first act shows Bianca first acting as a docile gentle girl, then showing scorn toward her sister and raising her voice—only to turn back to face a suitor in a sweet and submissive manner. This version depicts her not only nearly as angry and "untamed" as her sister, but as a girl who is falsely cordial—to her own advantage. From this, it is questionable whether or not she and Katherine were truly polar to begin with. Later, in act two, Bianca makes reference to all the things she has (making certain to mention those are the things that Katherine lacks). She is of course tied up by Katherine; however, telling your captor all the reasons you're better then them doesn't seem like a very effective escape strategy. It's fairly obvious that this is some twisted and extreme sibling rivalry, wherein both Katherine and Bianca behave like shady brats. In other words, Bianca is, to some degree, insulting in the same way that Katherine is.*

It would be unfair to only address Bianca's ambiguous personality and not even mention Katherine's multifaceted character traits. She is a very vocal character, tossing out wit whenever an opportunity arises; however, after Petruchio sexually assaults her then announces their alleged engagement, she remains silent. Yet again this is a scene with endless possibilities for interpretation, but when just reading through the lines it seems clear that Katherine may just be compliant after all—or even just wants love after all. The inconsistencies in her personality are proof that she isn't entirely shrewish—it seems all the more possible that she has a mental illness causing her to have severe violent outbursts rather than just a hate towards literally everyone. It seems as though she isn't just at the far end of the patriarchal spectrum of women's personalities after all.

Evidently, neither of them measure up to the roles that they are seemingly reversing by the end of the play. However, it seems that neither of them had swapped attitudes but that they'd instead just portrayed a different element of their personalities that weren't highlighted previously in the play. After all, women don't have a single, two dimensional mood, but react in different ways to different things as any normal person does. To think that either of them only possess a single demeanor that are complete opposites—simplifying Katherine's abusive and violent behavior to disobedience by even comparing

Bianca's shift in character with her "role"—is very small minded indeed. Not only is it ludicrous to compare Bianca's exercise of her free will with Katherine's maltreatment of people in general, but it's also preposterous to assume that Katherine has changed herself rather than just obeying her husband out fear of him. One can see that someone with Katherine's rage couldn't just be domesticated so easily—which shows that she most likely hasn't changed at all. Additionally, Bianca didn't quite show any shrewish traits other than not coming at her husband's beck and call, which doesn't scream demon wench, does it?

It's clear that Katherine and Bianca haven't just reversed roles. Neither of them are consistently polar from each other (they are sisters after all) and both show similarities at times. The idea that they swapped roles entirely is distinctly absurd to say for sure. However, this is a play and there is many different ways to interpret everything and this works in the favor of anyone with a brain and an imagination—therefore creating the most comfortable opportunity to argue this point with ease. The point being that an analysis of this piece evidently shows the elasticity in these sisters' attitudes.

Each of these student samples demonstrates the development of a claim, the use of well-chosen, integrated quotations to support that claim, and the synthesis of material from multiple sources.

SUMMARY

This chapter has demonstrated how to actively engage students of all ages in the study of Shakespeare by drawing attention not to the Shakespeare-iness of Shakespeare, but the similarities to Shakespeare's language, thoughts, and conflicts to their own lives. Additionally, this chapter shows how to concretely address the "Shakespeare specific" Common Core standards of comparing two or more performances of the same play without simply burning two or three days of class time with watching a movie, as well as addressing how to teach Shakespeare's use of allusions.

Finally, students will leave this unit with an appreciation of omission. Because this is a text with so many interpretations, as well as a play that shows us the power of performance as a deception, students will learn to support their analysis with examples from the text. Their reasoning must be thorough, thoughtful, and effective. Has Katherine been tamed? Are we all performing? Students will understand that it is not just what authors leave on the page for us to understand, but what they very purposely leave off.

Chapter Five

Teaching *Hamlet*

Or, How to Approach the Most Important Piece of Literature Ever Written

UNIT QUESTION: HOW DO YOU KNOW WHAT YOU KNOW AND WHAT HAPPENS IF YOU DON'T?

INTRODUCTION

It's troubling to hear teachers say, "These kids can't handle (insert title here)." It's something one hears a lot. And it's something one hears too often when talking about Shakespeare. The assumption that students who are below grade level can't appreciate Shakespeare is problematic for many reasons, but the one that we're going to have to deal with immediately is that Shakespeare is the *only* specifically mandated author in the Common Core standards.

Like everything else in this text, this chapter is not meant to be a template. Take what would work for your students, adjust to your audience as necessary, but, before you start making graphic organizers and worksheets, may we humbly suggest that the reason Shakespeare is still relevant today is the widely agreed-upon fact that he is the voice of human complexity—his high drama feels familiar, intense, and interpersonal. Let it be complicated for your students because the subject matter *is* complicated. They'll appreciate their teacher's refusal to "dumb down" a challenge.

This chapter will demonstrate strategies for, when approaching the teaching of a text, determining the purpose in teaching that text and identifying explicitly what skills you want students to develop through the study of that text. The chapter also establishes a rationale for the teaching of Shakespeare, even the most complex of his plays. It will demonstrate how teachers should not shy away from complex works for even their struggling students, as these texts are often the most relevant to the student population.

Additionally, this chapter will provide "ways into" the play that can be the basis for student analysis. Finally, the chapter provides a plethora of assessment possibilities, which include lists of possible content material that the teacher may use as their basis of the "backwards map" for the teaching of the unit.

COMMON CORE STANDARDS ADDRESSED

✍ College and Career Readiness Anchor Standards for Reading 6–12

1. Read closely to determine what the text says explicitly and to make logical inferences from it; cite specific textual evidence when writing or speaking to support conclusions drawn from the text.

2. Determine central ideas or themes of a text and analyze their development; summarize the key supporting details and ideas.

3. Analyze how and why individuals, events, and ideas develop and interact over the course of text.

> 9–10: Analyze how complex characters (e.g., those with multiple or conflicting motivations) develop over the course of a text, interact with other characters, and advance the plot or develop the theme.

4. Interpret words and phrases as they are used in a text, including determining technical, connotative, and figurative meanings, and analyze how specific word choices shape meaning or tone.

> 11–12: Determine the meaning of words and phrases as they are used in the text, including figurative and connotative meanings; analyze the impact of specific word choices on meaning and tone, including words with multiple meanings or language that is particularly fresh, engaging, or beautiful. (Include Shakespeare as well as other authors.)

5. Analyze the structure of texts, including how specific sentences, paragraphs, and larger portions of the text (e.g., a section, chapter, scene, or stanza) relate to each other and the whole.

6. Assess how point of view or purpose shapes the content and style of a text.

> 11–12: Analyze a case in which grasping point of view requires distinguishing what is directly stated in a text from what is really meant (e.g., satire, sarcasm, irony, or understatement).

7. Integrate and evaluate content presented in diverse media and formats, including visually and quantitatively, as well as in words.

11–12: Analyze multiple interpretations of a story, drama, or poem (e.g., recorded or live production of a play or recorded novel or poetry), evaluating how each version interprets the source text. (Include at least one play by Shakespeare and one play by an American dramatist.)

9. Analyze how two or more texts address similar themes or topics in order to build knowledge or to compare the approaches the authors take.

9–10: Analyze how an author draws on and transforms source material in a specific work (e.g., how Shakespeare treats a theme or topic from Ovid or the Bible or how a later author draws on a play by Shakespeare).

10. Read and comprehend complex literary and informational texts independently and proficiently.

WHERE TO BEGIN WITH A DIFFICULT TEXT

Here's one thing that should make a difference if you are anxious about reading Shakespeare with your students: avoid reading only for plot.

Because your students are now experts at close reading, they should be picking up and discussing foreshadowing and motifs and possible resolutions early on in the text. Discuss with them early and often that, when it comes to close literary analysis, plot is often secondary. Students should read the play to think about it, analyze it, and discuss it, not to figure out what happens next. Tell students on day one of the unit that *Hamlet* ends in a bloodbath with most everyone dead, including Hamlet. It's true. And it doesn't take anything away from their experience of studying the play.

In fact, for your lower-level students, having an idea of what is going to happen in advance is incredibly useful when they are struggling with the language of the text. Remember, a class that feels urgent, important, and busy, is a happy, well-behaved class. A class that is dragging, passive, and disengaged from you and the texts will not move forward in skill development.

STRUGGLING WITH THE LANGUAGE OF THE TEXT

Students don't need to understand every word of the play. Tell them it should be hard. Validate the struggle. And don't call on them to read aloud if you know they are really struggling (unless they volunteer). Instead, you can use short clips from stage and film productions, or you can model how to read the speeches yourself. If you want students to understand the play, they should hear it spoken with proper inflection by someone who already understands it.

As their comfort level increases, increase the level of participation. If students struggle with the reading of the text, do not let them off the hook for participation; rather, find different opportunities for them to engage in the text that don't include the reading of Renaissance English in front of their peers.

If at all possible, find various clips from stage and screen productions of the same scene. For instance, when teaching "To be or not to be," will you use Kenneth Branagh's version, wherein Hamlet knows he's being overheard? Or will you watch Richard Burton's version, which is the classic interpretation? Or Ethan Hawke wandering through a Blockbuster Video store, clearly drawing attention to the idea of life as a series of performances? It changes the motivation and the understanding of the diction within the scene. Let students view multiple versions of scenes (not entire movies, just scenes) and let them see professionals manipulate the language. Let them see how the performance lends itself to the analysis.

POSSIBLE LECTURES/DISCUSSIONS

In this Common Core unit of study, students will begin to understand and examine:

- Internal versus External Conflicts. For example, Hamlet's internal struggle to take action paired with the external conflict of Fortinbras marching on Denmark.
- Characterization, with emphasis on static and dynamic characters. For example, Horatio as a static character, versus Hamlet as dynamic. Why do both types of characters exist? What purpose do they serve? How do dynamic characters lead to a greater understanding of complexity within the text?
- Motifs. For example, the motifs of ears, rotting gardens, and fathers and sons.

What is the purpose of motifs? How do they serve the audience's understanding of a text? When and why are they used implicitly? Explicitly?

- Ambiguity in the Text. For example, the (purposefully?) ambiguous language providing multiple interpretations of the plot, such as when

Hamlet tells Ophelia to "get thee to a nunnery." Is this a pun on the word "nunnery," or should it be taken literally? Deciding on the interpretation changes the motivation of the scene. Why does Shakespeare leave this ambiguous? What is the power of ambiguity in this scene and others?
- Monologues and Soliloquies as Characterization. For example, *Hamlet* is an examination of self—existential universal questions are posed by the play. Using any of the seven major speeches in the text, how can students identify theme? Universal ideas? Mood? Conflict? Characterization? It's also a fun place to teach paradoxical arguments and existentialism if times allows.
- Universal Themes/Questions that arise in literature. For example, the theme of the impossibility of certainty. *Hamlet* examines the indistinct line between sanity and insanity. Spend time looking at critical moments in the text and discussing with your students whether Hamlet is *ever* insane. Is insanity something you can slip into and out of? Consider the closet scene with Gertrude. How about the fight in Ophelia's grave? Is he insane at the end? Was there always a method to the madness? Consider discussing how society treats people viewed as insane. If something is broken within, but we can't see it physically, it makes people extremely uncomfortable. Why?

Another theme in the play is betrayal. Spend some time working with the Rosencrantz and Guildenstern scenes. These are friends of Hamlet's who are spying on him, being disloyal. This is a familiar problem to teenagers. When does Hamlet realize they are lying? How do we know? And most importantly, what does it do to a person to have to question *all* of their personal relationships?

Yet another theme is the loss of faith. Hamlet questions his faith and the religious implications of his actions, but he also loses faith in his relationship with Ophelia, with the loyalty of his mother, with the friendship of Rosencrantz and Guildenstern. Here is a great opportunity to discuss metaphysics and existentialism within the play, as well as the fluidity between Catholic and Protestant symbols in the play and their representation of the Reformation during Shakespeare's time.

This isn't a complete list—certainly there's room for more. Use *Hamlet* to examine basic concepts such as characterization; this text is ideal to demonstrate *why* these seemingly simple concepts matter and are more complex than they may seem.

When preparing to teach any iconic text, consider downloading university lectures from iTunes U to play for your students. They're free, and just about always amazing. All levels of students can gain exposure to the level of rigor from the best universities in the country, and they begin to realize they can keep up! This is a wonderful way to practice note taking, prepare students for college and career, and give first-generation college-bound students a glimpse of what awaits them at a university and prove to them they are ready for the challenge.

HOW TO BEGIN

Start day one of *Hamlet* by playing Queen's "Under Pressure" while perhaps quickly and chaotically going through a slide show of images from past performances and quotes from the text. Students don't write anything down, they just absorb. We are opening the door to this world. Then, have students write in large letters as their first lecture note "Hamlet: Under Pressure." That is the premise with which we begin.

Throughout the unit, projects, and independent reading, continually come back to the idea of Hamlet acting from an immense pressure—spiritual pressure, psychological pressure, political pressure, familial pressure, and more. This idea of pressure is not new to students. They understand pressure well, and have a predisposition toward empathy for Hamlet because of it.

Taking It Further

Have students keep a running log of textual evidence for each type of pressure, and discuss how it pushes Hamlet toward action or inaction. This topic could even be the prompt for a writing assignment or a Socratic seminar.

CREATING CONCERN FOR HAMLET

Always paired with this pressure is Hamlet's struggle with the uncertainty about just about everything in his life. Because of all the upheavals around him, he is paralyzed with inaction because he just can't be sure of anything. As a highly intellectual character, he is terribly aware of the ramifications of making impetuous (and perhaps wrong) choices.

Activity—What Do You Know?

1. The following activity will allow students to truly appreciate this struggle, as well as provide a "way in" to the unit question, "How do you know what you know and what happens if you don't?"

Have students privately make a list of everything they are sure of in this world. Lists might include

- who loves them;
- what they have faith in; and
- what they value in this world.

These lists should come rather easily to students, as the questions are based around their very sense of self. And then, ask the questions: How do you know? How are you *sure* of any of this? How do you know your mother loves you? What is your proof? What if, when you were almost twenty-eight years old, she turned to you and said, "I was faking it." What would that do to your world?

The goal is for students to recognize that their identities rely on a degree of certainty about things in their lives, and (more importantly) if they (like Hamlet) lost certainty in these things, their worlds would seem to crumble. It would be devastating.

This activity also introduces the theme of the impossibility of certainty—a concept easy to grasp, but hard to appreciate. What would happen to us if we no longer could trust anything in our worlds? What does constantly living with uncertainty do to a person?

By the end of this activity, students are empathetic to Hamlet, prepared to appreciate his conflict and distrust of everyone (especially the women) of the play, as well as ready to appreciate the motif of ears and spying within the text. These ideas are no longer just things to memorize, but personal to them as well.

A RETURN TO CLOSE READING

Remembering that we've already studied and practiced the skill of close reading; the first question for your class is simply this: What does the first line of the play ("Who's there?") tell us? You can expect responses like:

- It's dark.
- It's spooky.
- The setting is unsure.
- It creates a mood of suspense.

And more. Lead the conversation toward the idea that the play begins by making us unsure of even the most basic questions around us.

This idea, paired with the idea of working under immense pressure, should guide students to the emotional chaos of not just Hamlet, but the entire state of Denmark. Students need to appreciate that Shakespeare crafts a play that strips certainty not just from our protagonist, but from the people of Denmark. By beginning the reading of the play with a simple close read of its first line, students will feel empowered and encouraged to work with such a difficult text. They'll know that they can do it.

If students continue to struggle with the opening of the play, validate the struggle. It isn't that Shakespeare is necessarily hard to read, it's that exposition is hard. No one ever says this, but it's true. Have you ever read twenty pages of a book and then abandoned it? Have you ever fallen asleep in the first twenty minutes of a movie? That's because, though the guts of the piece may be incredibly interesting, getting there can be boring. When you aren't emotionally invested yet, you don't know who is who or why they are who they are, and it can be easy to tune out. If nothing else, acknowledging that exposition is more difficult is often enough to get students to stick it out with you.

FINDING CHARACTERIZATION IN THE CHOICES

Another way to create interest and engagement in the opening scenes of the play is to take some time to decipher the emotional state in which we meet our protagonist, Hamlet. The scenario: Hamlet's father, the king, recently deceased. Hamlet's mother newly married to her brother-in-law, Hamlet's uncle. Worse, much worse, we see that the new couple is happy together and has strong sexual chemistry. Hamlet must bear witness to all of this.

Activity—Hamlet's First Line and First Soliloquy

Ask students to raise their hand if they are from some type of combined family—half sisters, brothers, stepparents, or stepsiblings. Many will raise their hands. The rest are familiar enough with the concept of blended families to empathize. Ask them if the "new guys," as it were, ever felt like interlopers in their family dynamic. When Claudius reprimands Hamlet for still grieving, discuss not only how obnoxious that is, but how enraging it would be that your stepfather is telling you to get over the death of your biological father. The students, right away, are on Hamlet's side. This allows a discussion of Hamlet's first line, "A little more than kin and less than kind." Why is it an aside? What does that tell us about our main character?

This discussion will lead students to recognize:

- that he is not a confrontational person;
- that he is witty;
- that he is uncomfortable with his uncle and mother;
- that he is unhappy; and
- that he is isolated and marginalized within his family and the court.

Take these inferences and guide students through Hamlet's first soliloquy. Compare initial ideas from his first line with those of his first speech. Have students annotate a copy of the speech. Underline images, circle hyperbole, highlight allusions. Have them create a map of the language that leads us toward:

- A mood for Hamlet—how does he feel?
- An initial understanding of Hamlet—what is he like?

Below-grade-level students are just as able to do this as higher achieving students—and the skill level remains high. From this point, move into a discussion evaluating why we, the audience, meet Hamlet once he is in an emotional crisis. What do we do, how do we act, when we are in an emotional crisis? Does it change how we behave? All of this creates a complex understanding of Hamlet *before* the true conflict of the play is introduced.

ANNOTATING MAJOR MOMENTS

In-class preparation throughout this unit should include a variety of pivotal passages (both speeches and dialogue) that students can annotate individually or in small groups. Remember to reinforce the idea that annotation is not merely labeling literary devices, but a chance for students to *interact* with the text and see connections that are demonstrated in that piece of text as well as with the text as a whole.

There are many schools of thought about how to grade annotations. Some teachers prefer a color-coded key that differentiates different literary terms. If your student population would benefit from an explicit strategy for annotation, that should be fine. Annotations, however, are never the end of an activity. They are the tool we use as an aid in preparing commentary. It seems most important to make sure it is thorough, and students are proving they are seeing connections between lessons, lectures, literary terms, and the text.

The next step should be a close-read response. Figure 5.1 is an example of an annotation followed by a short-answer close-read response of Hamlet's

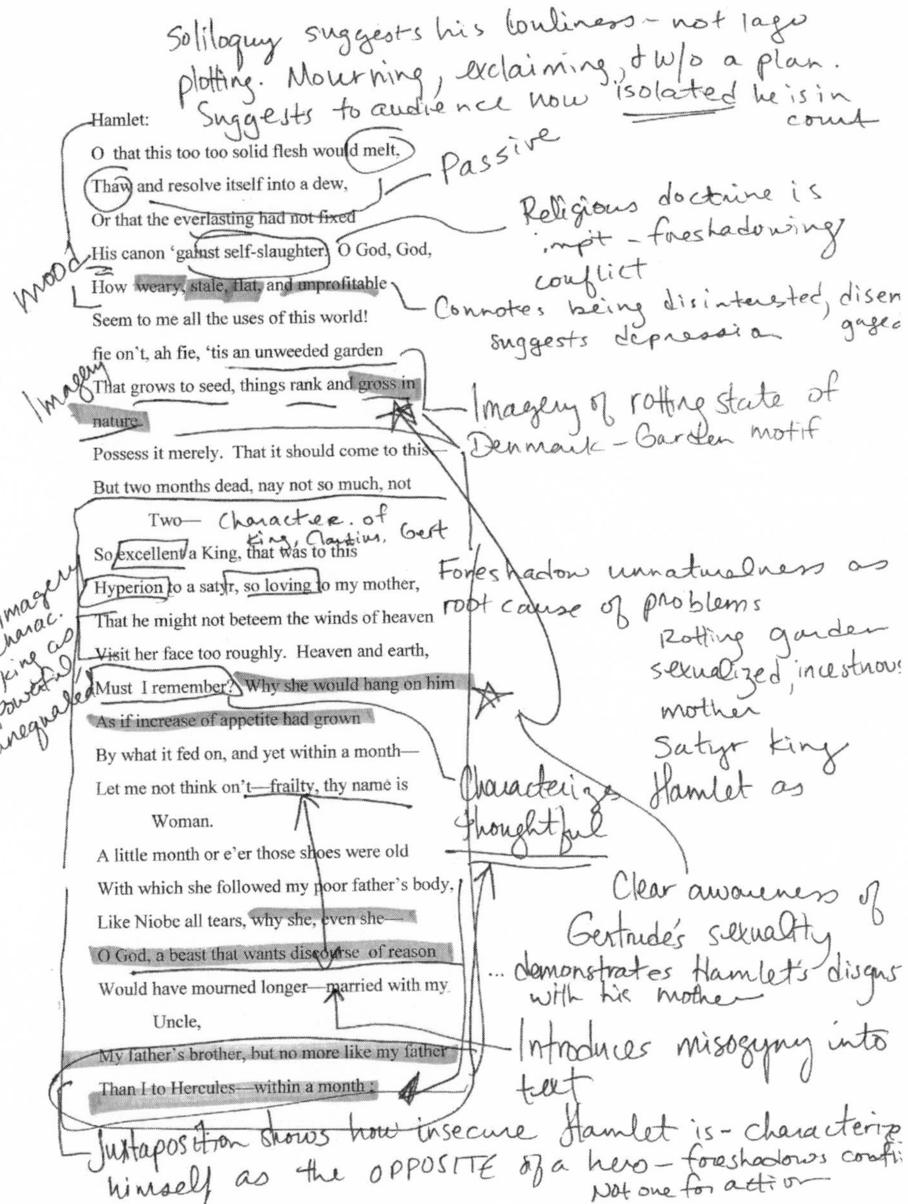

Hamlet:

O that this too too solid flesh would melt,
Thaw and resolve itself into a dew,
Or that the everlasting had not fixed
His canon 'gainst self-slaughter. O God, God,
How weary, stale, flat, and unprofitable
Seem to me all the uses of this world!
fie on't, ah fie, 'tis an unweeded garden
That grows to seed, things rank and gross in
nature
Possess it merely. That it should come to this—
But two months dead, nay not so much, not
Two—
So excellent a King, that was to this
Hyperion to a satyr, so loving to my mother,
That he might not beteem the winds of heaven
Visit her face too roughly. Heaven and earth,
Must I remember? Why she would hang on him
As if increase of appetite had grown
By what it fed on, and yet within a month—
Let me not think on't—frailty, thy name is
Woman.
A little month or e'er those shoes were old
With which she followed my poor father's body,
Like Niobe all tears, why she, even she—
O God, a beast that wants discourse of reason
Would have mourned longer—married with my
Uncle,
My father's brother, but no more like my father
Than I to Hercules—within a month ;

Soliloquy suggests his lonliness - not Iago plotting. Mourning, exclaiming, & w/o a plan. Suggests to audience how isolated he is in court
Passive
Religious doctrine is impt - foreshadowing conflict
mood
Connotes being disinterested, disengaged suggests depression
Imagery
Imagery of rotting state of Denmark - Garden motif
Character. of King, Claudius, Gert
Foreshadow unnaturalness as root cause of problems
Imagery charac. king as powerful unequaled
Rotting garden sexualized, incestuous mother
Satyr king
Characterizes Hamlet as thoughtful
Clear awareness of Gertrude's sexuality
... demonstrates Hamlet's disgus with his mother
Introduces misogyny into text
Juxtaposition shows how insecure Hamlet is - characterizes himself as the OPPOSITE of a hero - foreshadows confli
Not one for action

Figure 5.1.

first soliloquy after the entire text has been studied. Teachers could elect to do a pre- and post-close read—one immediately after the study of the speech, then one after the entire text has been read. What did they pick up on the first time? On reflection of the entire text, why is the speech significant to the play as a whole?

Notice that the annotations on the textual excerpt are in line with the content of the close read. Not everything is included, but you can see how the one leads to the creation of the other. Student interaction with the text is evident—that should be the grade in the grade book.

Sample Close-Read Response

Diction throughout the first soliloquy of Hamlet establishes for the audience what Shakespeare wants us to immediately understand about the characterization of major characters.

Hamlet's opening lines long for something to make him disappear, rather than taking violent action against himself. The diction of "melt" and "thaw" suggest a longing to disappear rather than a willingness to take his own life. The connotation of "thaw" and "melt" suggests something slow and natural—so slow, one would hardly notice it happening. They are calm words, the verbs are passive. An action that happens, not an action that is forced to happen. This shows us something immediately about Hamlet that is going to force him into conflict later in the text: he does not seek out action or confrontation.

This is reinforced with the conclusion of the speech, which ends, "But, break my heart, for I must hold my tongue." Why must he? This demonstrates to the audience that Hamlet, in the beginning of the text, is depressed and disgusted with the state of Denmark, but has no desire to challenge the state of things.

The soliloquy also compares Denmark to an "unweeded garden" which introduces the garden motif within the play. This is significant because the motif works to compare Denmark to a fallen Garden of Eden. This image, paired with others (for instance, King Hamlet being poisoned while sleeping in his garden, as well as the famous line, "Something is rotten in the state of Denmark") all lead toward the biblical allusion of a fallen Eden as a motif in the text. This allusion creates an allegiance between Hamlet and the audience and the dead King Hamlet. Claudius and Gertrude are unnatural, are part of the fall of Eden, and the memory of King Hamlet is the memory of a paradise on Earth.

The soliloquy also strives to point the finger of blame on Gertrude, not Claudius. She is the "frail" woman whose beast-like sexual appetite has embarrassed her son. Most of the disparaging language within the text like "beast," "appetite," "wicked," and "incestuous sheets" are focused only on her. This introduces the motif of misogyny within the text, and helps to foreshadow Hamlet's preoccupation with both his mother's and Ophelia's sexuality. Additionally, it establishes immediately that Hamlet sees Gertrude's behavior as unnatural. This theme of the unnatural actions of Claudius and Gertrude causing the "rot" of the state will be carried throughout the text. Finally, it shows that Hamlet, the son, is emotionally abandoned by his mother after the sudden death of his father, characterizing Gertrude as (at best) thoughtless, and a terrible mother who is prioritizing her own pleasure over her son's needs.

The most important aspect of this soliloquy is how it establishes the major players within the text. The dead King Hamlet is characterized with diction such as "excellent," "hyperion," and "loving" all of which establishes a hero worship between the father and son. As previously mentioned, it also introduces the motif of King Hamlet being associated with Denmark when it was a paradise. All of this makes King Hamlet godlike to his son; King Hamlet is held up as the example of greatness, but he also serves to demonstrate how Prince Hamlet sees himself and his uncle as his father's opposites.

Most tellingly, when Hamlet says, "married with my uncle, my father's brother, but no more like my father than I to Hercules," Hamlet tells the audience that in the exposition of the text, Hamlet sees himself as the opposite of the hero, Hercules. This image shows us he is not a man of action or heroism. Interestingly, in this comparison, Hamlet associates himself with his uncle rather than his father. Because it is clear he has no admiration for his uncle, this further suggests to us that Hamlet begins the play feeling unworthy. This is important because as the play unfolds, his feelings of self-loathing and self-doubt will create barriers to taking action.

Prince Hamlet establishes himself within the course of the soliloquy as highly cognitive; he's a thinker. Phrases such as, "Must I remember?" and "But break my heart, for I must hold my tongue" both demonstrate that Prince Hamlet thinks deeply about the world around him and feels powerless to effect positive change in conflicts that seem larger than him.

Additionally, the very fact that Hamlet has so many soliloquies helps to establish him as a highly cognizant character. He will not engage in open verbal conflict with Claudius or Gertrude, even when baited, in act 1, scene 2, but rather waits until he is alone to verbalize and articulate his problems to himself and by himself. This reinforces the idea of him being more intelligent than those around him and also shows us that at the beginning of the play, Prince Hamlet is desperately lonely. This apparent desperation helps us understand why he may be so willing to believe the ghost of his father when he appears.

This is important because it foreshadows the major conflict of the play: Can Prince Hamlet, no more like his father than he is like Hercules, do what his godlike father sends him to do and take vengeful action against his uncle, the king? Shakespeare begins the text explaining to us that even though the young prince sees everything that is wrong around him and it breaks his heart, he has no intention of challenging it. He begins this play as an entirely passive character that will be forced to become active in a world he has come to despise.

We created the sample close-read response above to show how a student may use literary terms effectively, incorporate textual evidence, and show understanding of how theme and conflict are being introduced within the text. Using only one page from the play, the student can demonstrate a depth of knowledge that demonstrates college and career readiness.

If you were to provide the above as an exam, consider having students write on top of their passage in big letters: "*So what?*" and "*This is important because*". . . . Hopefully, by having those two reminders in front of them, they will avoid merely labeling examples of literary terms in their annotations and will instead work on articulating *how* the literary choice they are seeing employed by the author lends itself to larger goals of the text as a whole.

For example, the repeated animal/sexual imagery attributed to Gertrude in this initial soliloquy is no mistake. The imagery allows the audience to infer that Hamlet is disgusted with his mother, which foreshadows the theme of unnaturalness within the text. The words "beast," "appetite," "wicked," and "incestuous" are there on purpose to set the stage for a theme of the entire text. Students need to move past simply applying the term, and toward seeing how the application of the term changes our understanding of the play.

Activity—Close-Reading Group Project

✍ In addition to meeting Common Core Anchor Standards for Reading, the following activity also addresses several anchor standards in Speaking and Listening:

College and Career Readiness Anchor Standards for Speaking and Listening 6–12

1. Prepare for and participate effectively in an range of conversation and collaborations with diverse partners, building on others' ideas and expressing their own clearly and persuasively.

2. Integrate and evaluate information presented in diverse media and formats, including visually, quantitatively, and orally.

4. Present information, findings, and supporting evidence such that listeners can follow the line of reasoning and organization, development, and style are appropriate to task, purpose, and audience.

To provide practice with useful annotations and close reads, consider the following activity prior to a close-reading exam:

1. Assign small groups (no more than four students per group) and give all groups the same passage from the play.
2. Provide students with 10–15 minutes to annotate the passage completely.
3. Elect/call on one member of each group to show their group's annotation on the document camera. Each group explains why they annotated what they did. Because it is visible to all, other groups can add on to their original annotations.
4. After all groups have contributed their annotations, allow 20–30 minutes for students to create a group close read.

By the end, students will have the support of a small group for the initial annotations and the first written response, as well as the support of the whole class's annotations. It will benefit students to see what other people saw in the same excerpt that they had.

The exercise will demonstrate to students all the different possibilities of the same twenty or so lines. Students of all abilities are being challenged and engaged, and the teacher is facilitating their learning, rather than lecturing. This allows the teacher to gauge how well the skills are being mastered.

This exercise is excellent preparation for a close-read exam and can be reused throughout the unit at other pivotal points in the text.

ASSESSMENTS AND BACKWARDS MAPPING

When discussing the opportunity to teach something as complex and multifaceted as *Hamlet,* it's hard to know what to include in a unit of study and what could be left behind. What follows is a range of assessment possibilities that include important moments from the text, discussion of motifs and themes, and interpersonal character dynamics. Consider what follows to be a place to begin the creation of your backwards map of the unit—decide what is most important to you and your students and let those be your lessons and discussions in the day-to-day presentation of information within the unit.

It may be helpful to choose one major type of assessment (timed writing, formal essay, close-read exam, short-answer exam, or Socratic seminar) after each act of the play. By the end of the unit, students will have had five major grading opportunities and experienced a variety of assessment styles, all of which are rigorous and student driven—no bubbling required.

Writing Timed Responses

✍ College and Career Readiness Anchor Standards for Writing 6–12

9. Draw evidence from literary and/or informational texts to support analysis, reflection, and research.

10. Write routinely over extended time frames (time for research, reflection, and revision) and shorter time frames (a single sitting or a day or two) for a range of tasks, purposes, and audiences.

It is important that assessments at the high school level mirror the university exam-sitting experience from time to time. Teachers need to vary their type of assessments throughout the year to ensure that they are proper preparation for what lies ahead for the students. One assessment option that could work with any text is a timed writing that combines formative and summative understanding. That is, a combination of quotes to be analyzed alongside short questions to which the student responds in essay format. For example:

1. Describe, in detail, Hamlet's relationship with women throughout the play.
2. What purpose does the gravedigger serve?
3. Annotate the speech. Explain, in detail, its relevance to our understanding of the play:

> *There's a special providence in the fall of a sparrow. If it be now, 'tis not to come. If it be not to come, it will be now. If it be not now, yet it will come—the readiness is all. Since no man of aught he leaves knows, what is 't to leave betimes? Let be.*

4. Is Hamlet insane?
5. Annotate the speech. Explain, in detail, its relevance to our understanding of the play:

> *Here is your husband; like a mildew'd ear,*
> *Blasting his wholesome brother. Have you eyes?*
> *Could you on this fair mountain leave to feed,*
> *And batten on this moor? Ha! have you eyes?*
> *You cannot call it love; for at your age*
> *The hey-day in the blood is tame, it's humble,*
> *And waits upon the judgment: and what judgment*

Would step from this to this? Sense, sure, you have,
Else could you not have motion; but sure, that sense
Is apoplex'd; for madness would not err,
Nor sense to ecstasy was ne'er so thrall'd
But it reserved some quantity of choice,
To serve in such a difference. What devil was't
That thus hath cozen'd you at hoodman-blind?
Eyes without feeling, feeling without sight,
Ears without hands or eyes, smelling sans all,
Or but a sickly part of one true sense
Could not so mope.
O shame! where is thy blush?

Just five questions. If only an hour was allotted, require them to write on no more than three, possibly two. Notice that the test is deceptively simple—one page, five questions—but it will require an immense amount of work on the student's part.

Group Presentation

✍ College and Career Readiness Anchor Standards for Speaking and Listening 6–12

1. Prepare for and participate effectively in a range of conversation and collaborations with diverse partners, building on others' ideas and expressing their own clearly and persuasively.

5. Make strategic use of digital media and visual displays of data to express information and enhance understanding of presentations.

6. Adapt speech to a variety of contexts and communicative tasks, demonstrating command of formal English when indicated or appropriate.

The prompts that follow can be used for the creation of a rigorous and engaging project that requires groups to defend and support a specific claim:

Group 1: Hamlet is insane. Prove it.

Group 2: Hamlet is sane. Prove it.

Group 3: Hamlet moves between sanity and insanity. Prove it.

OR:

Group 1: Give a ten-minute lesson on why Hamlet resonates with the question of humanity.

Group 2: Give a ten-minute lesson about the Catholic and Protestant undertones in the play.

When grading group assignments, make sure your rubrics are grading the *skills* from the unit. Sometimes group presentation rubrics pad the student grade with things that don't matter nearly as much as the quality of the content. In order to keep momentum in the classroom, and keep your unit moving forward with urgency, consider utilizing the following strategies for the rest of the class during group presentations:

- Have students take notes, ask questions, and/or write a reflection for each group presentation they witnessed. Have that type of participation be part of their overall grade.
- At the end of the group presentations, tell them they may use their notes on a test you've created based on content from the group presentations.
- Have a prompt that is specific to one group, and have the whole class write on it.

Whatever you do, the goal is that *all* students be engaged throughout the entire process. Otherwise, you should not devote so much class time to something that only applies to four or five students at a time.

Essay Topics for *Hamlet* Unit

✍ College and Career Readiness Anchor Standards for Writing 6–12

1. Write arguments to support claims in an analysis of substantive topics or texts, using valid reasoning and relevant and sufficient evidence.

2. Write informative/explanatory texts to examine and convey complex ideas and information clearly and accurately through the effective selection, organization, and analysis of content.

5. Develop and strengthen writing as needed by planning, revising, editing, rewriting, or trying a new approach.

When studying a complex text such as *Hamlet*, it will be important to provide opportunities for students to embrace the complexities of the text. In written form, the best way to allow students to truly explore the depth of the play would be to allow opportunities for full-process essays. Each of the topics below will provide opportunities for students to examine the complexities of the text, as well as the opportunity to consult other literary criticism about the text for research purposes.

- Watch two productions of *Hamlet* and compare and contrast two major scenes. What choices did each production make that altered your interpretation of the text?

- Hamlet states "Denmark is a prison." Write a paper discussing how that statement works as a metaphor throughout the text.
- Pick a soliloquy from *Hamlet* and choose three literary terms to discuss within that soliloquy. For instance, for the "To be or not to be" speech, you may choose theme, imagery, and characterization. Write an essay about how Shakespeare utilizes those three terms within your chosen soliloquy.
- One interpretation of the text is *not* that Hamlet is unable to act, but rather that he *chooses* not to act until he has gathered all information. This represents the theme of the impossibility of certainty. Write an essay discussing how Shakespeare develops this theme in the text, and what it suggests to the reader.
- Explain how the ear motif, spying, and the human need for privacy interplay with each other within the text.

Socratic Seminar

✍ College and Career Readiness Anchor Standards for Speaking and Listening 6–12

3. Evaluate a speaker's point of view, reasoning, and use of evidence and rhetoric.

4. Present information, findings, and supporting evidence such that listeners can follow the line of reasoning and the organization, development, and style are appropriate to task, purpose, and audience.

Provide students with a list of possible Socratic seminar topics toward the beginning of the unit. Students should be told that throughout the study of the text, special attention should be paid to these particular topics. This will force them to take better notes and approach the reading of the text with particular questions in mind.

Socratic seminars are wonderful because they reinforce the often-neglected Speaking and Listening standards of the Common Core, as well as provide an excellent chance for the teacher to gauge their level of understanding about the text. Socratic seminars keep the impetus on the student to effectively interact with the text, the lectures and discussions, and their peers.

A teacher should always feel free to abridge or add on to these topics. Just remember to choose questions that are complex and without one simple answer. Also, the questions should demand a familiarity with the text and any skill-specific concepts you want to make sure are being tested. Always require textual evidence to support their stance.

1. Is Ophelia sympathetic? To whom did she owe her loyalty?
2. How does Hamlet's self-loathing affect the progress of the play?
3. The critic Harold Bloom once described Shakespeare's *Hamlet* as "the invention of the human." What do you think he means? Do you agree?
4. How is *Hamlet* a play about familial responsibility? How is Hamlet reacting to:
   • the pressure of being a great man's son;
   • the discomfort of feeling more intelligent than one parent;
   • feeling disappointment in the character of his mother;
   • challenging figures of authority in his life?
5. How/why does Shakespeare leave the question of Hamlet's sanity ambiguous?
6. What is the purpose of including Rosencrantz and Guildenstern within the text?

The Close-Read Exam

✍ College and Career Readiness Anchor Standards for Reading 6–12

1. Read closely to determine what the text says explicitly and to make logical inferences from it; cite specific textual evidence when writing or speaking to support conclusions drawn from the text.

4. Interpret words and phrases as they are used in a text, including determining technical, connotative, and figurative meanings, and analyze how specific word choices shape meaning or tone.

✍ College and Career Readiness Anchor Standards for Writing 6–12

9. Draw evidence from literary and/or informational texts to support analysis, reflection, and research.

What follows is an option for a final exam for this unit of study that is based entirely on excerpts from *Hamlet*. These should be excerpts you've explicitly studied in class, but also they should cover a myriad of different aspects of the text.

Directions: Please choose two passages from the options below.

- Step one: annotate your chosen passage completely.
- Step two: write a one-to-two page (minimum) analytical close-read response discussing the significance of each of your chosen passages.

The following is a list of potential passages for use in this exam (line numbers are from the Folger edition of the play):

- Act 1, scene 5, lines 49 to 116 (the Ghost's speech)
- Act 3, scene 1, lines 113 to 141 (the "Get thee to a nunnery" scene)
- Act 3, scene 3, lines 40 to 76 (Claudius's speech)
- Act 5, scene 1, lines 133 to 160 (the Gravedigger scene)

In an exam such as this, students have to prove their understanding of the content of the literature as well as demonstrate their depth of understanding about the skills practiced throughout the unit. They are interacting with the text and creating their own analytical, timed responses. All of this will aid in preparation for Common Core exams, as well as mirror a university exam experience.

The Short-Answer Exam

✍ College and Career Readiness Anchor Standards for Writing 6–12

1. Write arguments to support claims in an analysis of substantive topics or texts, using valid reasoning and relevant and sufficient evidence.

9. Draw evidence from literary and/or informational texts to support analysis, reflection, and research.

What follows is another final exam possibility that again emphasizes students demonstrating a summative understanding of skills and content covered in the unit. Students will have to incorporate effective examples from the text, as well as compose logically cohesive and persuasive arguments. Again, this exam demonstrates the extent to which assessments should always be student driven. A student can't fake these answers. To succeed, they will need to have a depth of understanding from the unit of study. This, too, is excellent preparation for Common Core exams.

Student Instructions

Choose 3 of the following topics to write a short (1 or more pages) analytical response. Include literary terms and examples from the text for full marks.

- Explain the significance of ears as an extended metaphor in the play.
- Explain the significance of Denmark as a rotting body.
- Explain the significance of being lied to/spied on.
- Explain the idea of the contemplative side of Death in the play.
- Explain the significance of Gertrude and Hamlet's relationship.
- Explain the significance of Hamlet and Claudius's relationship.

This cumulative test is entirely written, covers a vast majority of knowledge, and requires students to apply the skills they've learned in the unit.

They don't need to memorize any facts, and they can't guess the answers. Like the Common Core assessments, this exam requires students to create and execute their own argument in writing.

The Final Paper

If, at this point in the year, you feel your students would benefit from another process-paper opportunity, consider what follows. The essay prompts each require students to interact with the text by providing persuasive evidence for their thesis. All topics will demand analysis paired with strong written construction.

Student Instructions

Choose one the following topics and write a 3–5 page paper. Papers must be typed, using Times New Roman 12-point font, be double-spaced, with a 1-inch margin. Note: the topic below is not your thesis; you must develop a thesis around the topic.

1. Discuss the significance of the play beginning with a question ("Who's there?").
2. Discuss the five-act structure, using *Hamlet* as an example.
3. Discuss the significance of a play within a play.
4. Discuss the significance of the line, "Something is rotten in the state of Denmark."
5. Discuss the significance of the line, "A little more than kin and less than kind."
6. Discuss Shakespeare's use of character foils in the play.
7. Discuss the relationship between Hamlet and Claudius.
8. Discuss the relationship between Hamlet and Gertrude.
9. Discuss the relationship between Hamlet and Ophelia.
10. Discuss the role of soliloquy in the play.
11. Discuss the possibility of a Freudian reading of the play (Oedipal Complex).
12. Discuss the role of doubt/uncertainty in the play.
13. Discuss the ear motif.
14. Discuss possible reasons for Hamlet's hesitation/slowness in taking revenge.
15. Discuss Ophelia and her role in the play.
16. Discuss the prison motif.
17. Discuss the significance of the "To Be or Not to Be" soliloquy.
18. Discuss the significance of the gravedigger scene, both in terms of comic relief and of its effect on Hamlet.

19. Discuss the significance of the "fall of a sparrow" speech.
20. Discuss the significance of Fortinbras having the last line of the play.
21. Discuss the significance of Hamlet's final words ("the rest is silence").

Here, again, the onus is on the student. Also, note that the rigor of the assessments closely aligns itself to what will be expected for students to be college and career ready. They must compose their argument, provide textual evidence to support their stance, and present it logically and persuasively to an audience. The stakes are high for them.

Also note that students are provided with a multitude of possibilities about what to write on. This avoids trapping them into failing because they didn't study/understand/review that one crucial thing. Instead, students can pick what they are most interested in with regard to content and still demonstrate their mastery of the skill. This will serve them better on the Common Core assessments, and will create a bought-in, focused classroom that is fostering a curiosity about literature.

SUMMARY

This chapter has demonstrated that teachers should never shy away from difficult texts, but rather embrace them as perfect opportunities to teach major literary skills such as ambiguity, characterization, and theme.

Notice, in this chapter, that the content of *Hamlet* is always at the forefront, but that all lessons, lectures, and assessments apply high-level skills to the engaging, iconic content.

Students have . . .

- practiced annotating using all their literary terms;
- applied those annotations to a written close-read assignment that allows them to practice engaging in the text;
- supported their writing with details from the text; and
- practiced cooperative group work with high stakes that demand the ability to apply skill to the text and the comments of the other students participating.

We have also demonstrated a myriad of assessment possibilities that cover a wide range of Common Core ELA (English Language Arts) anchor standards, while remaining highly engaging and challenging for students of all abilities.

Finally, we looked at how to present assessments as urgent for all students in the room and how to emulate the university-level experience via lessons, lectures, and exams.

Chapter Six

Teaching Fiction Writing

The Importance of Allowing Students to Create, Revise, and Publish

UNIT QUESTION: WHAT MAKES A STORY GOOD?

INTRODUCTION

This chapter will present strategies for teaching fiction writing to middle and high school students. The strategies in this chapter are based upon trial-and-error efforts to address the most common fatal mistakes in student fiction: weak conflicts (or lack thereof), underdeveloped scenes (or lack thereof), unrealistic dialogue (or lack thereof), and quick, way too easy resolutions (or lack thereof).

Though it represents one of only three types of writing assignments in the Common Core standards, creative writing often takes a back seat to expository and persuasive writing, at least in regard to the amount of focus it receives in the classroom. It has been our observation, though, that teaching creative writing with a true focus on technique and depth of knowledge has the after effect of creating more critical readers who are more aware of techniques being employed and significant choices being made by authors.

Through the study of various works of contemporary short fiction and the creation and revision of multiple works or their own, students will demonstrate proficiency in the techniques and craft of fiction writing.

COMMON CORE STANDARDS ADDRESSED

✍ College and Career Readiness Anchor Standards for Reading 6–12

3. Analyze how and why individuals, events, and ideas develop and interact over the course of a text.

5. Analyze the structure of texts, including how specific sentences, paragraphs, and larger portions of the text (e.g., a section, chapter, scene, or stanza) relate to each other and the whole.

10. Read and comprehend complex literary and informational texts independently and proficiently.

✍ **College and Career Readiness Anchor Standards for Writing 6–12**

3. Write narratives to develop real or imagined experiences or events using effective technique, well-chosen details, and well-structured event sequences.

5. Develop and strengthen writing as needed by planning, revising, editing, rewriting, or trying a new approach.

Table 6.1 displays the specific techniques that the Common Core standards expect of students when writing narratives (there are quite a few) and also demonstrates the progression of those expectations from eighth to twelfth grades.

"FIESTA, 1980" BY JUNOT DÍAZ

Several activities in this chapter include examples from contemporary fiction writer Junot Díaz's short story "Fiesta, 1980." Díaz won the 2004 Pulitzer Prize in fiction for his novel, *The Brief Wondrous Life of Oscar Wao*. He currently teaches creative writing at the Massachusetts Institute of Technology. "Fiesta, 1980" can be found in Díaz's 1996 short-story collection, *Drown*, a book that we have had to repurchase several times over the years, as students often ask to borrow it after reading one of Díaz's stories.

WHY WE ASSIGN CONTEMPORARY SHORT FICTION, AND WHY YOU SHOULD, TOO

If you have a student population that is really struggling with the basics of reading and writing, let alone discussing literary techniques used in literature, consider the wonders of the contemporary short story.

The following unit has been taught in high-achieving magnet classes and in remedial English courses alike. It works for a few very simple reasons:

- If you have a low-level group of students, you probably also struggle with things like attendance and tardiness. Perhaps there is a large swath of your class you only see three times a week. If that describes you, the short

Table 6.1. College and Career Readiness Anchor Standard for Writing #3 (italics added to demonstrate progression of the standard—notice that the differences between 9–10 and 11–12 are subtle but significant, requiring greater depth of knowledge).

8	*9–10*	*11–12*
3. Write narratives to develop real or imagined experiences or events using effective technique, relevant descriptive details, and well-structured event sequences.	3. Write narratives to develop real or imagined experiences or events using effective technique, *well-chosen* details, and well-structured event sequences.	3. Write narratives to develop real or imagined experiences or events using effective technique, well-chosen details, and well-structured event sequences.
a. Engage and orient the reader by establishing a context and point of view and introducing a narrator and/or characters; organize an event sequence that unfolds naturally and logically.	a. Engage and orient the reader by *setting out a problem, situation, or observation, establishing one or multiple point(s) of view*, and introducing a narrator and/or characters; *create a smooth progression of experiences or events*.	a. Engage and orient the reader by setting out a problem, situation, or observation *and its significance*, establishing one or multiple point(s) of view, and introducing a narrator and/or characters; create a smooth progression of experiences or events.
b. Use narrative techniques, such as dialogue, pacing, description, and reflection, to develop experiences, events, and/or characters.	b. Use narrative techniques, such as dialogue, pacing, description, reflection, *and multiple plot lines* to develop experiences, events, and/or characters.	b. Use narrative techniques, such as dialogue, pacing, description, reflection, and multiple plot lines to develop experiences, events, and/or characters.
c. Use a variety of transition words, phrases, and clauses to convey sequence, signal shifts from one time frame or setting to another, and show the relationships among experiences and events.	c. Use a variety of techniques *to sequence events so that they build on one another to create a coherent whole*.	c. Use a variety of techniques to sequence events so that they build on one another to create a coherent whole *and build toward a particular tone and outcome (e.g., a sense of mystery, suspense, growth, or resolution*.
d. Use precise words and phrases, relevant descriptive details, and sensory language to capture the action and convey experiences and events.	d. Use precise words and phrases, telling details, and sensory language to *convey a vivid picture of the experiences, events, setting, and/or characters*.	d. Use precise words and phrases, telling details, and sensory language to convey a vivid picture of the experiences, events, setting, and/or characters.
e. Provide a conclusion that follows from and reflects on the narrated experiences or events.	e. Provide a conclusion that follows from and reflects on *what is experienced, observed, or resolved over the course of the narrative*.	e. Provide a conclusion that follows from and reflects on what is experienced, observed, or resolved over the course of the narrative.

stories are great because a student with attendance problems *is not left behind the class because they missed the previous day's reading.*

A student who misses a lot of class can still come in and get a complete literary experience that is interesting, engaging, and done, start to finish in fifty minutes. It takes away the student's ability to disengage because they haven't been in class. More importantly, it allows the teacher to demand 100 percent engagement from everyone in the room, keeping expectations high.

- Unlike poetry, which can feel abstract and riddle-like (especially to low students, but sometimes to us all), short stories demonstrate skills necessary to the study of literature, but the narratives are far more straightforward and *easily comprehended.*

  Because of this, your below-grade-level students aren't shutting down because they are reading slowly—language is in their vernacular, length is manageable, and the arc of the story is clear. This takes away so much stress from the struggling student who may be trying to simply decode most of the lesson!
- Using contemporary short fiction also allows you a quick and effective opportunity to remediate skills that may not have been mastered with longer, less accessible texts. Revisit close reading with short stories to discover theme, inference, motif, characterization, and so on. These techniques are much more easily seen in the compact short story.
- Because the short story goes so quickly, the instructor can take this opportunity to fill this unit with voices that are compelling and engaging, but not often seen in high school reading lists, like those of Junot Díaz, Lorrie Moore, George Saunders, and Tobias Wolff. Using this medium opens up tons of options for literary style, voice, and aesthetics that students would not otherwise see. This exponentially increases the chances that you'll have more readers leaving your classroom who feel like the written word has something to offer *them.*

The next time you have a class that you feel will struggle with a longer text, consider a unit on contemporary short fiction where the voices may sound familiar, the conflicts may resonate, the choices might stun, the confidence of your students will rise, and the rigor stays just where you want it to be.

✍ In addition, the College and Career Readiness Anchor Standards for Reading calls for students to "grapple with works of exceptional craft and thought," including "high quality contemporary works."

SOME THOUGHTS ABOUT PLOTS (AND SOME NEW DEFINITIONS)

At the center of a good short story, and of any good work of fiction, is its conflict. At the middle and high school levels, conflict is typically defined for students as *the problem in the story*. This definition, as it pertains to helping students write good fiction, is neither complete nor effective. First of all, a story can have many problems, but not all of those problems are the conflict. Even the more specific and equally common definition—the *main* problem in the story—is problematic, as it leads students to believe that as long as their "conflict" is a problem for their character, it is suitable, which is not the case.

The strategies that follow are based upon the premise that conflict in a story is *what the protagonist wants*. Teaching the elements of plot as they relate to the protagonist's *desire* results in better student stories—better in multiple ways, not just better plotted stories. These "elements of plot" include *exposition, rising action, climax,* and *resolution,* and the following subsections will provide a definition for each element along with strategies for teaching them.

Exposition

The exposition of a story can be divided into two key components: ground situation and inciting incident.

Ground Situation

The ground situation is the "normal" state of things as the story begins. This is prior to the existence of the conflict, though there certainly can be "problems" in the ground situation.

Inciting Incident

The inciting incident is an event that changes the ground situation and results in the protagonist wanting something. Once this incident is established, the story has a conflict, a protagonist, and an antagonist.

The protagonist is the character struggling against the conflict.

The conflict is what the protagonist wants and the reason(s) he or she can't have it.

The antagonist is the reason the protagonist can't have what he or she wants—this antagonist can be person or thing, concrete or abstract, internal or external.

An effective way to explain these definitions to students is by using Pixar films (effective because these films are generally well plotted and because most students are familiar with them). Take *Finding Nemo*, for instance. The ground situation is that Nemo lives with his father, Marlin, in a coral reef. Nemo's mother and siblings are dead. We also learn in the ground situation that because of the death of Nemo's mother and siblings, Marlin is overly protective of Nemo, creating in Nemo, naturally, a bit of an adventurous streak.

The inciting incident occurs when Nemo is captured and taken away on a boat. This inciting incident changes the ground situation (Nemo no longer lives with Marlin on the coral reef) and results in the protagonist (Marlin) wanting something (to find Nemo).

Students may mistakenly suggest that Nemo is the protagonist of the film. In this situation, point out that the film is titled, *Finding Nemo*, and that the plot is driven by *Marlin's* desire to find his son. The film does, however, have a subplot, in which Nemo struggles to get out of a fish tank and return to his father. In this case, Nemo is the protagonist of the subplot, and this subplot, like the main plot, is instigated by the inciting incident.

There are many other examples that can be used to introduce this concept to students. In the film, *Wall-E*, for example, the inciting incident is the arrival of Eve, resulting in Wall-E's desire for . . . well, Eve.

Wall-E presents a common subcategory of inciting incidents, in which the ground situation is disrupted by the arrival of the protagonist's love interest. This type of inciting incident is apparent from *Romeo and Juliet* to *Twilight*. Students familiar with *Romeo and Juliet* may recognize a sub-subcategory, in which the protagonist initially desires Person A (ground situation) until the arrival of Person B (inciting incident).

Activity—Practice Identifying Inciting Incidents

Once ground situations and inciting incidents have been introduced to students, a great activity is to put students into groups and ask them to identify the ground situation and inciting incident of any book or movie. Sharing these out allows the class to hear several new examples and allows the teacher to check for understanding of the concept.

It is important to also discuss the extent to which conflict can be simultaneously internal and external (as opposed to simply one or the other) and how internal and external conflict can play off one another. Let's take another look at Marlin. His internal conflict, already present in the ground situation, is his fear of losing Nemo. This fear *causes* the inciting incident, as it is precisely Marlin's overprotective behavior that pushes Nemo toward the boat that will whisk him away. So Marlin's internal conflict causes the external conflict, and it is precisely his internal conflict that must be overcome to resolve the external conflict. At the story's end, Marlin must overcome his fear of losing Nemo in order to get him back.

This also demonstrates another aspect of conflict that students should understand: the conflict exposes the *themes* of the story. In the case of *Finding Nemo*, a theme is learning to trust one's children and let them go.

By the end of the exposition, it should be clear to the reader, at the very minimum, who the protagonist is, what the conflict is, and who/what the antagonist is.

Exposition in "Fiesta, 1980"

The short story "Fiesta, 1980" provides a more subtle (and literary) example of these elements of exposition. The ground situation is fairly simple: a family of five (Papi, Mami, Rafa, Madai, and the narrator, Yunior) is living in New Jersey, having emigrated from the Dominican Republic. The inciting incident occurs when Papi purchases a new van, resulting in both an external and an internal conflict for Yunior.

The smell of the new upholstery in Papi's car makes Yunior throw up (external conflict), but Yunior's rides in the new van with his Papi represent the only moments when he feels a bond with his abusive father, a fact that is complicated when on one of their "drives" Papi takes Yunior to the home of his mistress (internal conflict). As we will discuss in the following sections, these conflicts run parallel throughout the story, ultimately colliding in the story's climax.

Rising Action

In the rising action of a story, the protagonist struggles to get what he or she wants (but repeatedly fails).

This is an incredibly vital part of a student's story, and it is incredibly difficult to do well. What is at stake is a story that is engaging and dramatic versus a story that falls flat or sags in the middle.

Basically, this is the part of the story in which the protagonist sets out in pursuit of the thing he or she wants. Until the story reaches the climax, the protagonist must continually fail and keep going, fail and keep going. When planning and drafting the rising action of their stories, students should be instructed to keep the following in mind:

1. Never forget what your protagonist wants. This desire is what will drive the story forward, so keep asking, "What will my character do next to get what they want?"

2. Be sure your character is *active*, not *passive*. A common mistake in student fiction is for the protagonist to stand still (figuratively, but sometimes literally) while events unfold around them that will decide the solution to their conflict. The protagonist must actively pursue the object of his or her desire. One way to approach your rising action is to continuously force your protagonist to make difficult decisions.
3. Don't be too nice to your protagonist. You may like them, and may therefore not want to hurt them or make them sad, but that is the route of bad fiction. Bury your protagonist in obstacles and complications. The drama comes from how the protagonist digs out.
4. The stakes should get progressively higher, and the scenes should get progressively more dramatic. Each step the protagonist takes should logically lead them to the next step, eventually leading to the climax.

In the case of "Fiesta, 1980," the story alternates between scenes in the narrative present and flashbacks. In the narrative present, Yunior is struggling with his external conflict, first desperately trying (and failing) not to throw up on the way to the party, and then having food withheld from him at the party to keep him from throwing up.

In the flashbacks, Yunior is battling with two contradictory but coexisting truths:

- His trips to the home of the Puerto Rican woman bring him closer to his father.
- His choice to not tell his mother about the affair feels like a betrayal.

Climax

The climax is the moment when the resolution is locked in. The protagonist either will get what he or she wants or won't; the result is now inevitable (though maybe not apparent) and inescapable.

Of all of our definitions, this one is probably the least helpful without a concrete example. One such example comes in John Steinbeck's *Of Mice and Men*. The protagonists (yes, you can have two) are George and Lennie. What they want is to earn enough money to buy a ranch of their own, and the reason they can't have it is that Lennie keeps getting into trouble, forcing them to move on to another town and another job.

The climax of the novel comes when Lennie accidentally kills his boss's daughter-in-law, whom readers know only as Curley's Wife. Lennie had done bad things before, such as killing mice and puppies and grabbing women's dresses, but nothing of this magnitude. His earlier mistakes were things that he and George could escape from (fail and keep going), but not this time. When Lennie kills Curley's wife, the resolution is inevitable and inescapable: George and Lennie will not get their ranch.

As stated earlier, the rising action is incredibly difficult to plan and draft, and the climax may be even more difficult. Students will require the support of good, time-tested options for writing a climax.

One suggestion that is usually helpful to students is to put their protagonist in a situation in which he or she must *choose* between the thing he or she wants and something else that he or she values. This must be a *high stakes* dilemma. There is no going back from it.

In "Fiesta, 1980," Yunior (depending on your interpretation of the story's final lines) also faces a dilemma. Does he participate in maintaining the status quo, keeping his family together, or does he tell his mother the truth and break the family apart?

Resolution

Quite simply, the resolution is the solution to the conflict.

Students basically have four choices when it comes to resolving their story's conflict:

1. The protagonist gets what he or she wants.
2. The protagonist doesn't get what he or she wants.
3. The protagonist doesn't want it anymore (wants something else instead).
4. We can't tell (ambiguous ending).

Remind students that this resolution should progress directly and logically from the story's climax. The goal is to generate a resolution that the reader did not expect but in hindsight was inevitable.

It is helpful to teach these plot terms with the visual aid of a plot curve, or plot triangle. Students will recognize, from such diagrams, that the downward side of the curve rarely travels down to the level from which the curve began.

There are two reasons for this:

1. The story should never completely return to the ground situation. Once the conflict has resolved, things have changed.
2. In most cases, there is more story building up to the climax than there is following the climax. Students should be aware that their resolution can come right on the heels of the climax, and that the climax and resolution can even be the same scene.

In "Fiesta, 1980," the climax and resolution occur simultaneously, in two short paragraphs at the end of the story:

> *We were on the turnpike, just past Exit 11, when I started feeling it again. I sat up from leaning against Rafa. His fingers smelled and he'd gone to sleep almost as soon as he got into the van. Madai was out too but at least she wasn't snoring.*
>
> *In the darkness, I saw that Papi had a hand on Mami's knee and that the two of them were quiet and still. They weren't slumped back or anything; they were both wide awake, bolted into their seats. I couldn't see either of their faces and no matter how hard I tried I could not imagine their expressions. Neither of them moved. Every now and then the van was filled with the bright rush of somebody else's headlights. Finally I said, Mami, and they both looked back, already knowing what was happening.*

This ending presents an example of choice number 4, an ambiguous ending. Students will recognize that there are two things that could potentially be happening here:

- Yunior is about to throw up.
- Yunior is about to tell his mother about the affair.

Students often struggle with this type of ambiguity. They want to know what happens, and the author should/must tell them. But students should be guided toward an appreciation that the ambiguity makes the ending stronger.

Once students have an understanding of these elements of plot and how they work, they can begin planning a story of their own.

PLANNING THE STORY

Activity—Creating a Protagonist

Before students can begin plotting their stories, they will need to develop a protagonist, and it is important that the students understand their protagonists deeply. A great way to start is by using a character questionnaire. The Gotham Writer's Workshop offers one on their website that is very useful in helping students develop great characters. The book *What If? Writing Exercises for Fiction Writers* also includes some great questions for character building.

Once students have generated a character, instruct them to do the two following things:

1. Describe a day in their character's life, from the time they wake up to the time they go to sleep. This should be a normal, boring, typical day. Let's say it's a Wednesday.

2. Describe the one thing (or person) that the character *wants* more than anything else.

These two character development activities will be helpful as students work toward plotting their stories, particularly when developing the conflict.

Activity—Completing a Story Planner

Once students have created protagonists and have comprehensive knowledge of their protagonists, they are ready to build a plot around that protagonist. Students should complete a planner like the one below, which requires students to give a brief description of each of the plot's elements. It is important to instruct students that the more specific their plan is, the better, and that anything in their initial plan may change at any time as they draft their story.

Short Story Planner

Exposition

Protagonist (main character):
Ground Situation (normal state of things as story begins):
Inciting Incident (something that CHANGES the Ground Situation):
Conflict (what the protagonist wants and the reason he or she can't have it):
Antagonist:

Rising Action/Complications

Setbacks/Obstacles that keep the protagonist from getting what he or she wants:
1.
2.
3.
(More optional)

Climax

The moment when it's locked in: the protagonist will get what he or she wants or won't; the resolution is inescapable:

Resolution/Denouement

The result: the protagonist gets what he or she wants or doesn't (or he or she doesn't want it anymore, or we can't tell):

Students should turn these planners in for review before they begin drafting their stories, allowing the instructor to give feedback on the planned plot. Typical feedback at this stage includes observations that the conflict is not high stakes enough, that the protagonist is too passive in the rising action and climax, or that either the climax or the resolution (or both) is too easy.

DECISIONS, DECISIONS

Once students have completed their planner and have been given feedback, they are instructed that they now have a *map*, but do not yet have a *story*. They have a fully labeled plot curve, but *plot* and *story* are not the same thing, the former being the sequence of events, the latter the presentation of that sequence, along with all of the *choices* that that presentation requires.

Now students must decide *how* to tell the story:

- Which details about their character will they reveal?
- How will they reveal those details?
- Where will they begin? (They can begin anywhere on the plot curve.)
- How will they pace their story?
- What point of view will they use? First or third person? Limited or omniscient?
- How will they make their narrator's "voice" unique?

Showing, Not Telling

The first decision to focus on is how the students will reveal details. The students will also need to consider which details to reveal. For example, all of the details about the protagonist that are included in the character questionnaire do not need to be explicitly included in the story. A common mistake in student fiction is to plop in a large paragraph somewhere in the first couple of pages that *tells* the reader everything about the character. A better approach is to carefully choose a handful (or fewer) of significant details that *show* the reader who the character is.

It is at this point that the students should be introduced to a basic commandment of fiction writing: show, don't tell. When writing fiction, it is better to *show* the reader something than to *tell* the reader something.

One way to *show*, not *tell,* is to use vivid, specific, concrete details. An example for students that is fairly easy to understand is the difference between the statement "Bob hates penguins" and "Bob kicked a penguin," the latter being a concrete detail—and action—that shows, or implies, what is told in the latter.

Activity—"Showing" Character Traits

To practice this, put students into groups and give them the following statement:

Betsy is spoiled; no matter how much her parents do for her, she is never satisfied.

Then instruct the groups to compose one to two pages that *show* what is told in the statement. Instruct students that they must not, at any point, explicitly state that Betsy is spoiled; rather, they must show it through her actions and dialogue.

For subsequent individual practice, students can *show* the following statement:

Bernard was optimistic. No matter what happened, he always saw the "bright side" of everything.

Pacing

Another way for students to show, not tell, is to use *scene* as well as *summary* (as opposed to only summary, which is common in student fiction). Besides determining how the student will reveal detail in the story, the use of scene will also address another of our aforementioned important decisions: "How will you pace your story?" To put it simply, *pacing* is how fast or slow the story is moving, and this pace is controlled, in part, by summary and scene.

Summary in a story is a relatively large amount of time described using a relatively small number of words. In other words: more time, fewer words. *Scene*, on the other hand, is a relatively small amount of time described using a relatively large number of words, or: less time, more words. Scenes are made up of *action* and *dialogue*.

Activity—How Much Time Passes?

To demonstrate, instruct students to read the following description, and discuss the amount of time (fictional time, not reading time) that passes:

Tom walked to the corner store, bought a half-gallon of juice, and returned home, stopping to speak to his neighbor Sam on the way.

The variables here are distance to the store, how busy the store is, and how talkative either Tom or Sam are, but typical responses should range from twenty minutes to an hour.

Now have students read the following and do the same:

"Hello, Sam," Tom said, leaning against the fence surrounding Sam's yard.

"Hello to you," Sam said.

"Nice day today."

"It sure is."

Sam set the rake he had been using gently on the ground and walked toward Tom.

Typical responses should be ten to fifteen seconds, the only real variables being speaking speed and the speed at which Sam sets down his rake. Students may point out that the amount of time that passes is comparable to the amount of time it takes to read the passage, which is exactly right.

The first passage, which is summary, covers thirty minutes to an hour in twenty-four words; the second passage, a scene made up of action and dialogue, covers ten to fifteen seconds in thirty-eight words.

Students should then discuss, first in pairs, and then as a class, the following questions:

- Why do we want to have control over the pacing of our story? Why speed it up and slow it down?
- What events of your story should be told in summary? In scene?

Ultimately, the goal is for students to understand that a story should not be told completely in summary or completely in scene (either of these options could be pulled off, but only with great skill) and that the most dramatic moments of their stories should be presented (at least in part) as scenes. This includes the inciting incident, parts of the rising action, and absolutely the climax.

Pacing becomes one of the ripest areas for revision of student stories. A common comment on student rough drafts is, "Make this a scene!"

Dialogue Rules

In order for students to effectively write scenes, they need a sound understanding of how to write dialogue, beginning with how to punctuate it. The rules that follow cover the most common student mistakes and can be distributed to students as a handout, but they should be explicitly taught, as well, and students will need to practice them. While receiving this instruction, students usually behave as if they know all of this already, and then proceed to make constant mistakes in their stories. Simply refer them back to these rules.

Rule #1: Start a new line and indent one-half inch *every time the speaker changes*.

[TAB]"I've got it," shouted Bob, waving his arms in the air [ENTER].
[TAB]"Got what?" asked Luke, clearly confused by Bob's strange behavior [ENTER].
[TAB]"I forgot," Bob answered. "Never mind."[ENTER]

Note: If your word processor automatically indents after you press ENTER, do not press TAB again (make sure you indent only one-half inch).

Rule #2: Use dialogue tags: he said, she said, blurted Mary, Mark announced.

Note: There is nothing wrong with using "said" over and over and over. They are everywhere on a page of fiction, but are usually not distracting, like the power lines and poles in your neighborhood.
Also, in a long section of dialogue between two characters, once you have established who is speaking, you have the option of dropping the dialogue tags. This, of course, wouldn't work with three or more characters, and it is always important that it is clear to the reader who is speaking.

Rule #3: When the dialogue tag comes before the quotation, place the comma after the tag, outside the quotation mark:

Jon asked, "Where's my stick of butter?"
Jon asked,[COMMA][SPACE][QUOTATION MARK] "Where's my stick of butter?"

Note: No space before the comma

Rule #4: When the dialogue tag comes after the quotation, place the comma inside the quotation mark before the tag, with a period after the tag.

"That's my butter," he cried.
"That's my butter,[COMMA] [QUOTATION MARK] [SPACE] he cried. [PERIOD]

Note: in this case, the "he" or "she" is always lower case.

Another example:

"Who am I?" she asked.
"Who am I?"[QUESTION MARK] [QUOTATION MARK] [SPACE] she asked. [PERIOD]

Rule #5: When the dialogue tag comes in the middle of a line of dialogue, one of the following is happening:

a. The tag is in between two sentences. In this case, the line should look like this:
   "I have a dog," said Jane. "That makes me better than you."
   "I have a dog,[COMMA] [QUOTATION MARK] [SPACE] said Jane.[PERIOD] [SPACE] [QUOTATION MARK] "That makes me better than you."[PERIOD] [QUOTATION MARK]
   Note: the second sentence must begin with a capital letter (That).
b. The tag is interrupting one sentence:
   "I also have two cats," said Jane, "that I've trained to sing and run errands."
   "I also have two cats,"[COMMA] [QUOTATION MARK] [SPACE] said Jane,[COMMA] [SPACE] [QUOTATION MARK] "that I've trained to sing and run errands."[PERIOD] [QUOTATION MARK]
   Note: the second half of the interrupted sentence does not begin with a capital letter (that).

Activity—Practice Punctuating Dialogue

To allow students practice with this, give groups the following paragraph, which is stripped of all punctuation and formatting, and ask them to apply their dialogue rules to it:

> mary asked should we go to the party or not I don't know answered sandra do you think it's a good idea it might be fun mary answered but then you know he'll probably be there yeah said sandra that's what I'm afraid of
>
> The correct answer should look like this:
>
> Mary asked, "Should we go to the party or not?"
>
> "I don't know," answered Sandra. "Do you think it's a good idea?"
>
> "It might be fun," Mary answered, "but then you know he'll probably be there."
>
> "Yeah," said Sandra. "That's what I'm afraid of."

Subtext

Discuss with students that the purpose of dialogue is not only to reveal information—it can also reveal character—and that dialogue that is only used to provide information needed to move the plot along is often ineffective. Students should strive to make their dialogue sound believable. Encourage students to listen to as much dialogue as they can (without seeming too creepy). They will probably notice a few different things:

- People often do not speak in complete sentences.
- When two people are speaking, they do not take turns delivering blocks of dialogue while the other person waits quietly (there is usually much more give and take).
- People often do not say what they mean.

This last point leads into a discussion of a useful technique when writing dialogue: the use of *subtext*. Students will probably be familiar with the prefix *sub* and the word *text*, and so will be able to join you in arriving at the following definition:

SUBTEXT= the words beneath (or behind) the words

Students will probably also agree with you, if asked, that when people are having a conversation, they are not always saying exactly what they mean, and if students are asked to brainstorm examples of this, they can probably generate plenty.

Activity—Recognizing Subtext

To demonstrate how subtext works, ask students to discuss in pairs the meanings *behind* the following statements—what is *really* being said.

- "Are you going to wear that?"
- "Are you finished yet?"
- "Have you taken the trash out yet?"

Common responses, respectively, are as follows:

- "Don't wear that."
- "Hurry up."
- "Take the trash out now."

For older students, a great story to demonstrate an author's use of subtext is Ernest Hemingway's "Hills Like White Elephants."

Activity—Composing a Subtext Scene

To practice the use of subtext in dialogue, ask students to write a subtext-laden scene based upon the following prompt:

Two people are getting ready for a party. One thinks they look great, the other doesn't think so, and is trying to convince the first to change outfits.

For additional practice, use the following prompt:

Three people are talking. One is in love with one of the others. One is annoyed about something. The third is being polite, but wishes they were someplace else.

Flashback

Another technique that students can use to manipulate the pacing of their story is *flashback*. This technique can be used to pace the story and can also address another of our important decisions: "Where will you begin?" Flashback can allow the student to play with the order of events in the story, perhaps beginning the story *in media res* (in the middle of things).

A flashback is an interruption of *the narrative present* to show events that occurred at an earlier time.

The following is an example from "Fiesta, 1980"—the first of several flashbacks that Díaz includes in the story. Notice that Díaz indicates the shift in time in two ways: by separating the flashback with line breaks, and by beginning with the phrase, "the first time"

> *That was the end of the good times. Just outside the Washington Bridge, I started feeling woozy. The smell of the upholstery got all up inside my head and I found myself with a mouth full of saliva. Mami's hand tensed on my shoulder and when I caught Papi's eye, he was like, No way. Don't do it.*
>
> *The first time I got sick in the van Papi was taking me to the library. Rafa was with us and he couldn't believe I threw up. I was famous for my steel-lined stomach. A third-world childhood could give you that. Papi was worried enough that just as quick as Rafa could drop off the books we were on our way home. Mami fixed me one of her honey-and-onion concoctions and that made my stomach feel better. A week later we tried the library again and on this go-around I couldn't get the window open in time. When Papi got me home, he went and cleaned out the van himself, an expression of askho on his face. This was a big deal, since Papi almost never cleaned anything himself. He came back inside and found me sitting on the couch feeling like hell.*
>
> *It's the car, he said to Mami. It's making him sick.*
>
> *This time the damage was pretty minimal, nothing Papi couldn't wash off the door with a blast of the hose. He was pissed, though; he jammed his finger into my cheek, a nice solid thrust. That was the way he was with his punishments: imaginative. Earlier that year I'd written an essay in school called "My Father the Torturer," but the teacher made me write a new one. She thought I was kidding.*

Activity—Composing a Flashback

Instruct students to create a flashback (one page minimum) that explains Reynaldo's behavior in the following scene:

> As they approached, everything seemed fine. "What a beautiful day," she said, peering up at the blue sky, "Don't you think?"
>
> "I do. It is," answered Reynaldo, "A great day. I can't wait for the concert."
>
> Neither can I," she said, "It's going to be a blast. But we've got to eat. I'm starving."
>
> "So am I," said Reynaldo, "Where should we go?"
>
> "There's a place right up here," she answered.
>
> Reynaldo could hardly contain his happiness as he walked side by side with her up the busy street, but as they rounded the next corner, he suddenly stopped short. Looming over them were the all-too-familiar golden arches, and as Reynaldo's gaze lowered, he saw the sign: McDonald's.
>
> "No, no," Reynaldo muttered to her, "I can't."
>
> "What?" she asked with concern.
>
> "I can't go in there," he continued, "There's no way. I can't."

The following is a sample response to this activity from a tenth-grade student:

While she looked at him, expecting an answer, Reynaldo remembered that horrid day.

It was bright. His dad had decided to take him to the fair for his eighth birthday. His dad taking him somewhere was rare. Something told him it wasn't right, but what eight year old doesn't like the fair? So he went.

He recalled the awkward ride. His dad would try to ask him questions. Like how he was doing at school or if he had any trouble with his friends. He never liked how it sounded forced. Like his dad only talked to him as if nothing good was on the radio.

Before they arrived, Reynaldo asked to go to the bathroom somewhere. The ride was an hour long and his dad thought an eight year old wouldn't pee his pants. So, naturally, right when they got there, Reynaldo bolted toward the restroom, disregarding his dad. But on the way out, he noticed a clown blocking his view.

"Hey, kid. You lost?" He asked with a smile that made Reynaldo shudder.

"No, my dad's right there," Reynaldo lied, pointing to a man with his back turned.

"Here, I'll take you to him," the clown said, stepping forward.

"No, I could go myself."

In that instance Reynaldo sidestepped the clown, who reached for Reynaldo's wrist. Violently. Reynaldo found his dad screaming out his name to a crowd of people. Reynaldo ran toward him.

After that, he couldn't stand clowns. He covered his eyes at birthday parties. He vowed never to go to the circus. Even now, eight years later, he didn't look at clowns, and he knew it was irrational to blame his dad for the clown talking to him. He blamed him, anyway.

Narrative Voice

Not all narrators "sound" the same, just as not all people sound the same. In both cases, each individual has a distinct voice, and it is important—especially if the student is using a first-person narrator—that the story's narrator have a "narrative voice." Narrative voice is created by the *choices* the author makes and is often all mixed up with the author's *style*, which, to put it simply, is the accumulation of the author's choices.

Voice can be created by any or all of the following:

- Diction
- Repetition
- Figurative language
- Sentence structure

Analyzing Yunior's Voice

Yunior, the narrator of "Fiesta, 1980," has a distinct voice that is great for introducing this concept to students. Reread the opening paragraphs of the story (reprinted below):

> *Mami's youngest sister—my tía Yrma—finally made it to the United States that year. She and tío Miguel got themselves an apartment in the Bronx, off Grand Concourse and everybody decided that we should have a party. Actually, my pops decided, but everybody—meaning Mami, tía Yrma, tío Miguel and their neighbors—thought it a dope idea. On the afternoon of the party Papi came back from work around six. Right on time. We were all dressed by then, which was a smart move on our part. If Papi had walked in and caught us lounging around in our underwear, he would have kicked our asses something serious.*
>
> *He didn't say nothing to nobody, not even my moms. He just pushed past her, held up his hand when she tried to talk to him and headed right into the shower. Rafa gave me the look and I gave it back to him; we both knew Papi had been with that Puerto Rican woman he was seeing and wanted to wash off the evidence quick.*
>
> *Mami looked really nice that day. The United States had finally put some meat on her; she was no longer the same flaca who had arrived here three years before. She had cut her hair short and was wearing tons of cheap-ass jewelry which on her didn't look too lousy. She smelled like herself, like the wind through a tree. She always waited until the last possible minute to put on*

her perfume because she said it was a waste to spray it on early and then have to spray it on again once you got to the party.

We—meaning me, my brother, my little sister and Mami—waited for Papi to finish his shower. Mami seemed anxious, in her usual dispassionate way. Her hands adjusted the buckle of her belt over and over again. That morning, when she had gotten us up for school, Mami told us that she wanted to have a good time at the party. I want to dance, she said, but now, with the sun sliding out of the sky like spit off a wall, she seemed ready just to get this over with.

Next, discuss with students the following question: What creates Yunior's narrative voice?

Guide the students in recognizing all of the following elements that make up Yunior's voice:

- Colloquial language (slang, incorrect grammar) mixed with elevated, educated language
- Mild profanity
- Mixing of English and Spanish
- Sentence Fragments
- Similes

Yunior's voice is complex: for example, it is not simply the colloquial voice of a teen, but mixes those colloquialisms with the voice of an intelligent and perceptive young man.

Activity—Recreating Yunior's Voice

This time the damage was pretty minimal, nothing Papi couldn't wash off the door with a blast of the hose. He was pissed, though; he jammed his finger into my cheek, a nice solid thrust. That was the way he was with his punishments: imaginative. Earlier that year I'd written an essay in school called "My Father the Torturer," but the teacher made me write a new one. She thought I was kidding.

As practice in creating narrative voice, instruct students to write the essay, titled "My Father the Torturer," that Yunior would have written (as if the student is Yunior). The goal is to recreate Yunior's voice, employing all of the elements of his voice that the class identified earlier.

The following is a sample response to this activity from a tenth-grade student:

When other parents punish their kids, it's a time out. My jefé—my pops—he ain't no other dad. He could come up with a new way to punish you every week.

Like that time when I was five. I accidentally dropped a plate of beans and the plate shattered and the beans splattered everywhere like when you drop a water balloon. It's not like the plate was valuable or nothing. We had more in those run down cabinets we got. But nope, pops made me stand with a lemon straight off the comal pressed on my fingers. It hurt like the fire of a thousand suns. Moms couldn't do anything though. I don't blame her.

Recently, when I threw up in the car (long story, you don't wanna know), he made me stay on my knees for three hours. With my arms out. The old man told me, "Stay like that until I'm done cleaning." Then he finished and I was still on my knees. At one point it felt like little ants were biting my knees and were working their way up, poco a poco.

Those are just two of the pleasant ways my old man likes to torture me.

REVISION

✍ College and Career Readiness Anchor Standards for Writing 6–12

5. Develop and strengthen writing as needed by planning, revising, editing, rewriting, or trying a new approach.

Once students have made all of their "decisions" and have written a first draft of their story, it is important that this is not the *only* draft, as many of the author's most important decisions, and the most lasting lessons in craft, will come about in the second and subsequent drafts.

What is true for professional fiction writers is true for students: the writer needs to get as many different eyes on the draft as possible, allowing them to take in a wide range of feedback and reader responses.

In a classroom setting, this can be done in two ways:

- Peer Review
- Teacher Feedback

In first drafts of student short stories, the same problems persist that were mentioned earlier as possible feedback on the story planners: a passive protagonist, underdeveloped scenes (or summaries that should be scenes), low-stakes rising action and climax, and simple resolutions.

The following sample, from a tenth-grade short story, demonstrates a typical type of revision in student stories:

First Draft

Although she was angry at her mother, she was saddened and astonished by her mother's comment on her appearance. The result of the argument with her mother was beginning to wear on Sienna's confidence and her mother's comment continued to resonate with her. Also, a result of their argument, Sienna began to fast and limit herself to 1,200 calorie diet every other week for three months. Her weight loss began to show, and more and more people were beginning to complement her on her appearance. Although she continuously got positive feedback on her change in appearance, Sienna wasn't satisfied with herself. and her mindset hadn't changed.

The instructor comment on this paragraph was simply, "Can you show this?" The student's revision follows:

Second Draft

Although she was angry at her mother, she was saddened and astonished by her mother's comment on her appearance. The result of the argument with her mother was beginning to wear on Sienna's confidence and her mother's comment continued to resonate with her. Also as a result of their argument, Sienna began to fast and limit herself to 700 calorie diet every other week for three months.

"Have you lost some weight?" Mrs. Grayson asked, as she watched her daughter look at herself in the mirror.

"Does it look like I did?" said Sienna, snapping at her mother.

"Don't get smart with me," exclaimed Mrs. Grayson, "I was going to tell you, you look good."

"Oh my God, you're such a liar."

"I do not lie Sienna."

"Sure you don't, I know you see the billowing rows that line my back and the stretch marks growing up my sides," said Sienna, as she fell to her knees and started to bawl.

Instead of questioning Sienna, Mrs. Grayson got down on the floor with her daughter and held Sienna close to her.

"I'll never be like them," said Sienna, as the tears fell down her cheeks.

SUBMITTING STUDENT FICTION

Encouraging students to send out their work in pursuit of publication is an excellent way to improve student buy-in and to both justify and incentivize heavy and continuous revision. When students know that their teacher is not their only reader, the quality of student fiction seems to improve.

There are two ways to approach this:

1. Hold a fiction-writing contest at your school site. Accept blind submissions, recruit judges, purchase prizes, and hold a student reading for the winner and finalists. You may also be able to publish and bind the winning stories for distribution to your classes.
2. Help the students submit their polished stories to venues that publish fiction by young people. Two great options are the Scholastic Art and Writing Fair (www.artandwriting.org) and Teen Ink (www.teenink.com).

   In addition, the literary website New Pages has compiled a list of journals and websites that publish young writers. Their Young Authors Guide can be found here: www.newpages.com/npguides/young_authors_guide.htm.

FINAL ASSESSMENT

Fiction Writing Test

✍ College and Career Readiness Anchor Standards for Writing 6–12

3. Write narratives to develop real or imagined experiences or events using effective technique, well-chosen details, and well-structured event sequences.

Part 1:

Choose one of the following to respond to:

1. Discuss the extent to which *conflict* drives the plot of a story.
2. Discuss the importance of *pacing* in a short story, and how an author can control it.
3. Discuss the importance of *showing*, not *telling*, in a story and how it is accomplished.

Part 2: Punctuating Dialogue

Correctly punctuate the following:

is this your milk asked Charles which milk replied Ron this milk continued Charles in the huge gallon jug what about it asked Ron it takes up half of the top shelf in here responded Charles where will I keep my juice

Part 3: Showing, not Telling

Take the following statement and SHOW it (1 page minimum):

Samantha was nervous. She had to choose, and wasn't sure what was going to happen.

Part 4: Scene

Create a scene that includes both action and dialogue based on one of the following (1 page minimum):

- Two friends plan to shoplift something, but one backs out at the last minute.
- A friend is asked to babysit, but she really doesn't want to.
- A landlord and tenant disagree about the rent.
- Trying to end a conversation when the other person won't stop talking.

Part 5: Subtext

Explain in detail the subtext in the scene that you created for Part 4.

SUMMARY

Too often do we—especially in the later grades—give away the creative writing units in favor of something more "academic." This is absolutely backward, because a fiction-writing unit is the perfect platform for constant checking of understanding of literary concepts.

This chapter has demonstrated how to use quality short fiction to engage students in exploring the various elements of fiction. Not only are students applying this knowledge to the study of quality contemporary literature rarely seen at the high school level, but they are also employing these same techniques in their own short fiction. As all educators know, creation is higher on Bloom's Taxonomy than is recognition.

Throughout the unit, students are demonstrating their depth of knowledge by creating new fiction. Every creative task is grounded in skill development, but these assessments also serve to improve students' written voices, as well as their inherent appreciation of the craft of creating literature.

Chapter Seven

Slaughterhouse 5 and *The Things They Carried*

Appreciating Postmodern Approaches to Fiction

UNIT QUESTION: HOW DO YOU TELL AN UNTELLABLE STORY?

INTRODUCTION

The year after we first taught *Slaughterhouse Five* to tenth graders, a group of students was visiting after school. They were talking about their current English class, and a student said, "I'm really just more of a postmodernist than a modernist. Postmodernism is my thing." This interaction, besides being wildly rewarding, was a demonstration of one simple thing: too rarely do we expand our book lists past World War II and into experimental, postmodern fiction. When we do, we give room for students to realize there are all kinds of ways to tell their stories, and there is joy and adventure in finding the right fit for themselves and their writing.

This chapter will use Kurt Vonnegut's *Slaughterhouse 5* and Tim O'Brien's *The Things They Carried* to address the development of students' voice in their academic and creative writing, as well as demonstrate how to teach complex concepts such as postmodernism, metafiction, and experimentation with narrative style. It will demonstrate to students the importance of experimentation in fiction—that leaving the rules of "how it should be done" or "how it has always been done" behind allows for fresh storytelling and, in the case of both *The Things They Carried* and *Slaughterhouse Five*, reveals methods with which to tell a story that otherwise cannot be told.

COMMON CORE STANDARDS ADDRESSED IN THIS CHAPTER

✍ College and Career Readiness Anchor Standards in Reading

1. Read closely to determine what the text says explicitly and to make logical inferences from it; cite specific textual evidence when writing or speaking to support conclusions drawn from the text.

2. Determine central ideas or themes of a text and analyze their development; summarize the key supporting details and ideas.

4. Interpret words and phrases as they are used in a text, including determining technical, connotative, and figurative meanings, and analyze how specific word choices shape meaning or tone.

> 11th–12th: 4. Determine the meaning of words and phrases as they are used in the text, including figurative and connotative meanings; analyze the impact of specific word choices on meaning and tone, including words with multiple meanings or language that is particularly fresh, engaging, or beautiful.

5. Analyze the structure of texts, including how specific sentences, paragraphs, and larger portions of the text (e.g., a section, chapter, scene, or stanza) relate to each other and the whole.

> 11th–12th: 5. Analyze how an author's choices concerning how to structure specific parts of a text (e.g., the choice of where to begin or end a story, the choice to provide a comedic or tragic resolution) contribute to its overall structure and meaning as well as its aesthetic impact.

6. Assess how point of view or purpose shapes the content and style of a text.

9. Analyze how two or more texts address similar themes or topics in order to build knowledge or to compare the approaches the authors take.

> 11th–12th: 9. Demonstrate knowledge of eighteenth-, nineteenth- and early-twentieth-century foundational works of American literature, including how two or more texts from the same period treat similar themes or topics.

10. Read and comprehend complex literary and informational texts independently and proficiently.

WHAT IS POSTMODERNISM?

Postmodernism, as a cultural philosophy, is difficult to define, even for the experts, but there are common elements that unite works of postmodern *fiction* and that are beneficial for students to recognize and study.

Common characteristics of postmodern fiction:

- *Skepticism* about ideas or practices that society takes for granted, such as . . .
  - that stories have a beginning, middle, and end;
  - that nonfiction and fiction are two distinct genres;
  - that "true stories" are representations of reality; and
  - that fiction is made up, and therefore is not a representation of reality.
- As a result of this skepticism, a *rejection* of the traditional techniques and conventions of storytelling.
- In place of these rejected techniques, *experimentation* with new strategies for writing fiction; for example, metafiction.

Postmodernism in Tim O'Brien's *The Things They Carried*

Tim O'Brien's *The Things They Carried*, published in 1990, is a collection of related short stories (though, mistakenly, the book is commonly referred to as a novel) set in the Vietnam War and following Alpha Company, of which Tim O'Brien, also a character in the book, is a member.

The stories in the collection, viewed either individually or in relation to one another, display a postmodern approach to storytelling. In both *The Things They Carried* and *Slaughterhouse Five*, discussed later in the chapter, postmodern experimentation is used for the same reason: to find a way to tell a story that cannot authentically be told otherwise.

The following sections will provide strategies for teaching eight of the stories in the collection.

Title Story: Rejection of Conventions

"The Things They Carried," the title story and first story of O'Brien's collection, was first published in *Esquire* magazine in 1987. It is one of the most highly regarded American short stories of our time. It is also heavily anthologized (just try to find an anthology of American fiction or a creative writing textbook that doesn't include it).

What students will notice (or what they should be guided in noticing) when they read the story is that it is not like a typical story. It certainly has a plot: First Lieutenant Jimmy Cross is in love, but the girl he loves, Martha, sees him only as a friend (conflict). Despite this, Martha repeatedly does things that give Jimmy hope, such as signing her letters, *Love*. Martha sends Jimmy a pebble that she found, and he carries it in his mouth as a reminder of her.

On a patrol, Jimmy is distracted by the pebble and thoughts of Martha when one of his soldiers, Ted Lavender, is shot and killed. This is the story's climax. Jimmy feels intense guilt—he was not focused on his job and therefore feels responsible for the tragedy. In the story's resolution, he burns Martha's letters and resolves to focus on his duty.

But the story rejects traditional storytelling techniques in the presentation of this plot. The story's content, for the most part, is a long list of things that the men of Alpha Company carry—physical equipment side by side with abstract emotion. Jimmy's feelings of responsibility and guilt are simply two items on the list, much like his flashlight and canteen.

The "climax" of the plot is Ted Lavender's death; however, there is no rising action—no tension and foreshadowing-filled series of events leading up to the emotionally charged turning point. Instead, we are casually told of Lavender's death in the story's second paragraph, in a sentence that is not even about Lavender's death, but rather about the tranquilizers that he carried.

Activity—Tracking Ted Lavender

Instruct students to reread the story and keep a list of each time Ted Lavender's death is mentioned—in fact, in each case, have them write down the sentence or phrase that mentions it.

Students will discover that O'Brien tells the reader of Ted Lavender's death over and over again—three times in the aforementioned second paragraph alone. They will also discover that in most cases Ted Lavender's death is mentioned casually, offhand. Rarely is his being shot in the head part of the main clause of the sentence.

Now the important part: so what? Instruct students to discuss the significance of this choice. What is accomplished by it? What is the effect? Guide students toward recognition that the choice desensitizes the reader to Lavender's death—it is given no special significance and is thrown in early and often. There seems to be an emotional detachment to the event, for the narrator and the reader. Students may take this further and see the choice as a reflection of the qualities of war: death is everywhere in war—ingrained and embedded in war.

This would be a great time to introduce students to postmodernism. If students are unfamiliar with modernism, it may be wise to start there. Both modernism and postmodernism are complex topics, and the following is grossly oversimplified, but students should understand that modernism began in the early twentieth century and was a reaction to the unbelievable brutality of World War I, which included trench warfare, chemical weapons, and other advanced weaponry that destroyed too many young men of a single generation.

In the arts, modernism was a rejection of *romanticism*, which, in literature, features heroes, villains, supernatural beings, damsels in distress, and high emotion. Modernism also rejects *realism*, which is an attempt in the arts to "photocopy" real life.

After the brutal destruction of World War I, both romanticism and realism seemed trite and inauthentic. Life seemed meaningless, and there were no heroes. The philosophy of modernism was that there was no need to embellish or exaggerate or romanticize life; just tell it as it is. Also, trying to "photocopy" real life through art doesn't work. "Reality" is inside the individual mind. Postmodernism came about in the post–World War II era, encompassing the Cold War period and the Korean and Vietnam Wars. This era was defined by more death and more destruction, and the constant threat of nuclear annihilation.

Postmodernism is hard to define, which is kind of the point (life is hard to define). Even the smartest people on the planet have difficulty pinning down exactly what it is (possibly because in many ways we're still in the middle of it), but the descriptions given earlier in the chapter—centering on *skepticism*, *rejection*, and *experimentation*—can help students to make some sense of it. For the purposes of this unit, we want students to recognize and appreciate postmodern *choices* in fiction, and analyze the *effect* of those choices.

Postmodernism presents a challenge to modernism through the belief (fueled by skepticism) that there is no way to express *anything* remotely close to *reality*, even individual, subjective reality. The closest we can come, in art, is to gain some sort of understanding by throwing out the rules and experimenting.

In fiction, truth cannot be achieved by remaining organized or following rules (life isn't organized). Therefore, there is no need for a beginning, middle, and end. As a result, postmodern fiction is often filled with ambiguity. Postmodern fiction often avoids drawing neat conclusions or trying to make *sense* of things—in life, there are no real conclusions to be drawn.

Let's turn back to Ted Lavender and the question, posed to students, of the *effect* of the choice to reveal the story's climax offhand, almost as an afterthought, and to continuously repeat it in the same offhand manner.

The presentation of all of the story's content, Lavender's death included, as a list represents an experimental approach to storytelling, and gives the story a "flatness," in which every element, from the mundane (flashlight, canteen) to the monumental (death, grief, guilt, responsibility) exist on an equal level, reflecting the "truth" of war: death is daily/everywhere/ingrained. *Truth* in the previous sentence is placed in quotation marks because, as we will see in subsequent stories in *The Things They Carried*, a postmodernist would be skeptical of the meaning or even existence of "truth."

For additional stories that use a list as their organizing structure, try Lorrie Moore's "How to Talk to Your Mother (Notes)" or Ander Monson's "Dream Obits for Liz."

Love: Questioning the Reliability of a Narrator

O'Brien follows the twenty-six-page "The Things They Carried" with the three-page story, "Love," in which Tim O'Brien, the author as well as a character, visits Jimmy Cross many years after the war, and they reminisce about the events described in "The Things They Carried."

"Love" is the first of several stories in the collection that are an example of *metafiction*, a common experimental technique in postmodern fiction. Metafiction, quite simply, is writing fiction about writing fiction, or, to put it another way, fiction that is aware that it is fiction. The narrator of "Love" is the writer, Tim O'Brien, who in the story alludes to the writing of "The Things They Carried."

One of the most remarkable things about these two stories is the gap in narrative distance, forcing students to question the reliability of the narrator. "The Things They Carried" was narrated from an uninvolved, distant, third-person-omniscient point of view, whereas "Love" is narrated in first person from the perspective of the author (or the character representing the author), who is involved in the action of the story. "Love" in fact, includes in its opening paragraph a variation on the phrase, "the things they carried," in which the pronoun *they* is replaced with *we*.

Students should be aware that in any work with a first-person narrator, the reliability of that narrator should be questioned, as the narrator is a character and thereby subject to the flaws of any human being. But "Love" features particular elements that will force students to question the extent to which O'Brien is reliable.

In the entire twenty-six pages of "The Things They Carried," Tim O'Brien is never mentioned as a character—he never appears, but in "Love" we immediately discover that O'Brien was present for, and was a participant in, the events of "The Things They Carried." This seems like a significant omission, and students should be guided in a discussion of possible reasons for the choice.

Activity: Fiction or Nonfiction?

O'Brien presents "Love" as a true account. If you were to ask the students if "Love" is fiction or nonfiction, their immediate answer will probably be nonfiction, but three things should be pointed out to them:

- Flipping back to the book's title page, the collection claims to be a work of fiction. This could open up an engaging discussion with students: What is a story? Is "Love" a story? Is it truth or fiction? If it's not a story, what is a story?
- Through close reading, students will discover that portions of the story feature the descriptive techniques of a fiction writer—sensory detail, figurative language—so that what initially appears to be the author's account of what Jimmy Cross told him at Cross's kitchen table becomes clearly a fiction. Students will observe that it is highly unlikely that the description—given the level of detail—is entirely based upon O'Brien's memory of his conversation with Jimmy Cross. The "true story" is not reality, a concept that will prepare students for subsequent stories in the collection.
- Finally, the story ends with the narrator (who is also the author, who is also a character) openly conceding that he is not telling us the whole story, which runs counter to our expectations, as a reader, of a narrator.

How to Tell a True War Story: Questioning Truth and Reality

The sixth story in the collection "How to Tell a True War Story" will challenge students to defend their notions of what *truth* and *reality* are, as well as what a *story* is. A postmodernist would be skeptical of our ability to define any of these terms.

The following questions can be used to guide students' reading of the story (sample responses from a tenth-grade student are included):

1. What is the relationship between "reality" and "truth"? Are they the same things? Explain.

   The relationship between reality and truth in the story are that they are the same thing, but they are seen differently by people. Reality is not the same for everyone, so the story shows that there is no point in explaining something because no matter how many times you tell the story, there is always that surreal "seemingness," which makes the story untrue, when in fact it did happen.

2. Go back to the story Mitchell Sanders tells O'Brien, about the patrol in the mountains.

How does Sanders use the parts of the story that never happened to make the story more "true"?

Sanders sounded so confident and self-assured, who would doubt it was true? But good storytelling does not mean it actually happened. It's as if he had to add in what wasn't true to make it seem true.

3. Go back to O'Brien's story about the baby water buffalo.
   When we learn, at the end of the story, that this never happened, how does it affect you as a reader?

   One of the ideas behind postmodernism is that you can't get to "truth" in fiction by trying to recreate "reality" (because reality is so ambiguous it is impossible to recreate). So you have to come at the truth in some other way (maybe even through lies—like Mitchell Sanders).

   How does O'Brien use the story of the water buffalo to try to convey truth to the reader? What truth is he trying to convey?

   What does this reveal or suggest about the story of Curt Lemon's death?

   In the water buffalo story, O'Brien conveys truth by exaggerating every detail. The story shows the pain Riley went through when his best friend died, and that war is not always like the fun times they had. When I found out it never happened, it made me feel lied to. It starts with Riley writing an emotional letter about his best friend's death. How could you not feel bad for him? And then it was all a lie. Like O'Brien is saying, all you could say is "Oh" at the end of it. Maybe Curt Lemon didn't even die at all. It just made me doubt O'Brien all over again.

Through answering and discussing these questions, students should come to an understanding of O'Brien's argument in regard to the nature and purpose of stories: *truth* does not come from telling *what really happened* (a postmodernist would argue that such a thing does not exist); rather, the purpose of a story is to *convey* truth—to recreate for the reader a true experience (that may never have happened).

Students will initially struggle over these ambiguous and paradoxical concepts, but just keep the discussion going—they are worth struggling with.

"The Man I Killed," "Ambush," "Good Form"

The questions of fiction and nonfiction and truth and reality continue in a trio of stories: "The Man I Killed," "Ambush," and "Good Form." "The Man I Killed" and "Ambush" appear back-to-back near the middle of the collection, while "Good Form" appears several stories later, near the end of the book, but all three describe the same incident, and depending on your preference, you can pass on "Good Form" and use "Ambush," which immediately follows "The Man I Killed."

All three stories are quite short (seven, four, and two pages, respectively), and it can be very powerful to read all three aloud as a class (student reactions, after finishing the third story, generally range from shocked to angry).

"The Man I Killed" is about an enemy soldier that the narrator killed with a grenade. The "action" of the story consists of the narrator, Tim O'Brien, standing silently and staring at the man's body, as his friend Kiowa tries to console him and as Tim imagines the life this man may have led.

Activity—Examining Point of View

This is a great story with which to discuss choices in point of view. Ask students what point of view the story is in; they may initially respond that it is in third person, but upon further examination, they will see that, in fact, the story is told in first person. The reason for the confusion is that, despite being a first-person story, there are nearly no personal pronoun *I*'s in the story.

Students should then discuss the effect of that choice, coming to an appreciation that the narrator is passive in the story—he does nothing but stare—while the story itself is driven by the imagined life of the dead man.

The story is also riddled with repetition, the narrator repeating the same details about the man's damaged body numerous times. This is reminiscent of the repeated mentioning of Ted Lavender's death in "The Things They Carried," though students may recognize that the effect here is different: in "The Man I Killed," it is as if the narrator cannot escape the details of the man he killed—cannot stop staring and, over time, cannot stop recalling them.

In contrast to "The Man I Killed," the narrator of "Ambush," also Tim O'Brien, is *active*, and the story is a much more traditional first-person narrative, chronologically detailing the events that led to the killing of the enemy soldier. The story is emotionally engaging and powerful, but students will be mystified when they next turn to "Good Form" and discover that it never happened.

In "Good Form," O'Brien is author, narrator, and character all in one, and he claims that "Ambush" is *true* in the sense that it conveys an emotional truth—it recreates the essence of a true experience, but it is entirely made up. He never killed anyone, but he saw lots of bodies, though he never looked at them, and he feels guilt and remorse for those bodies. The story is an attempt to make the reader feel that guilt and that remorse.

O'Brien's final statement in "Good Form," that he can tell his daughter honestly that he had never killed a man and also honestly tell her that he had, is precisely the type of ambiguous and paradoxical concept that students should be wrestling with, and it will force them, as a postmodernist would prescribe, to reevaluate their ideas of what a story is and what truth is.

"Speaking of Courage," "Notes," "In the Field"

"Speaking of Courage" provides another opportunity for students to practice evaluating choices and their effect, particularly the choice of *repetition*, which we have seen previously in both "The Things They Carried" and "The Man I Killed."

Students should examine O'Brien's use of motifs in this story, of which there are several. A *motif*, quite simply, is something that repeats—pattern of repetition, often of an image or a symbol. For example, *doors* (open and closed) are a motif in the Disney film *Frozen*.

Remind students that when they look for motifs in a story, the goal is not only to identify the motifs, but also to examine what the motif implies or suggests (the *effect* of the motif).

Activity: Tracking Motifs

Instruct students to keep track of the following motifs in "Speaking of Courage":

- Time (pay attention to the constant references to time);
- Circles/Cycles/Roundness;
- Sinking/Movement downward;
- Speaking/Telling/Hearing/Listening;
- Stillness (not moving; stuck) vs. Movement (slow movement);
- Flatness/Smoothness.

The hard part, and the important part, will be putting together what the effects of these repetitions are. That's the "So what?"

"Speaking of Courage" is followed in the collection by the story "Notes," which is essentially the story of how "Speaking of Courage" came to be written and how it was heavily revised over the years. Like "Love," this story is *seemingly* a work of fiction, though according to the book's title page, the collection itself is a work of fiction. If "Notes" is a work of fiction, it is another example of metafiction.

In either case, "Notes" sheds an interesting light on both the story that precedes it ("Speaking of Courage") and the story that follows it ("In the Field"). In particular, the story's final sentence implies that the actions attributed in "Speaking of Courage" to Norman Bowker—and the guilt Bowker carries for those actions—actually belong to O'Brien.

The following questions can be used to guide students' reading of "Notes" (sample responses from a tenth-grade student are included):

1. What is your immediate gut reaction to reading this story?
   The last sentence got to me. So did the first paragraph, when it says that he killed himself, and then what his mom said, that he didn't want to bother anyone. I feel bad for the guy. He just wanted to tell his story, but didn't know the words. O'Brien is a sick freak if the last sentence means what I think, though.
2. In what ways does this story change your view of "Speaking of Courage"? Explain.
   It makes it seem more . . . planned. Norman wrote seventeen pages of just his thoughts, yet he never said it. Now he seems even more conflicted, to the point where he has nowhere to go, like in "Speaking of Courage." In a way, this story contradicts "Speaking of Courage" because it wasn't Norman's fault.
3. Is this story fiction or nonfiction? How do you know? Explain.
   Nonfiction! I think. It has parts of Norman's letter, unless O'Brien wrote the letter and then wrote the story about the letter. He doesn't seem to be telling much of a story.
4. Do we see any of the same motifs in this story that you saw in "Speaking of Courage"? Is the effect the same, or is it different? Explain.
   O'Brien tells the timeline of the drafting of the story, so in a way it reflects the motif of time. O'Brien doesn't seem to speak of courage, either. He writes about it. He explains the struggle he faced to get the story right, and Norman struggles with finding a way to put it. The effect is the same, except Norman never got to share it, or get it out. O'Brien was able to complete it.
5. What is your interpretation of the last line of the story?
   What it sounds like is that O'Brien was the one that let Kiowa's boot go. That's some messed up stuff. It's like "The Things They Carried" because although we know O'Brien was in the middle of the events, we do not know what part he had in it. It's once again as if he's hiding his part in it. Maybe Norman had a different story to tell, and O'Brien used it to include another of his own. Using a different name still leaves it the truth, though. Apparently it was just O'Brien that let Kiowa go.

In the Field

Students will use the story "In the Field" to examine *theme*, or an idea that applies not just to that story (or poem or play or novel), but also to the world outside of the story. In particular, this story demonstrates the theme of *blame*.

✍ College and Career Readiness Anchor Standards for Reading 6–12

2. Determine central ideas or themes of a text and analyze their development; summarize the key supporting details and ideas.

Activity—Tracking a Theme and Recognizing its Effect

The following questions can be used to guide students' reading of "In the Field" (sample responses from a tenth-grade student are included):

1. As you read, use sticky notes or a highlighter to track the development of the theme of *blame*.
2. In this story, O'Brien assigns blame for Kiowa's death in multiple directions. In your opinion, who is to blame? Why?
   The way the story is told, the boy (who I'm assuming is O'Brien) is to blame. The explosion happened when he turned on the flashlight, so the enemy could have noticed that.
3. Is there an overall "message" about blame in the story? What is it?
   The message seems to be that blame has to be given. Cross seems to have guilt because he was their leader. There is always a sense of guilt when bad things happen, even if one does not take direct action in it.
4. Does this story in any way contradict what we were told in "Speaking of Courage"?
   Somewhat, because in "Speaking of Courage," Norman blames himself, but in this story, he just seems sad that Kiowa is dead, not guilty at all. The blame isn't his only. It's everyone's.
5. Going back to the last line of "Notes": Do we gain any insight on that last line after reading "In the Field"? Explain.
   Yes, because if O'Brien is the boy, then it would explain why he blames himself for the death of Kiowa. He thinks if he hadn't turned the flashlight on Kiowa would be alive. Now we know what actually happened, unless he's lying again.
6. What is unique about the point of view in "In the Field"?
   It seems to be third and first person at the same time. O'Brien is the boy, so he is narrating the story, but it goes into the point of view of Jimmy Cross as well, kind of like in "Love".
7. What connections can we make between the point of view and the theme of blame?
   O'Brien doesn't say he is in the story. He is referred to as "the boy." When you feel guilt or blame for something, people often push it away because nobody wants to feel guilty. He gave the blame to someone else, not himself.

While studying these three stories, guide students toward an understanding that O'Brien tells us a *true* story—seemingly without telling us what *really* happened, indicating a struggle for O'Brien to tell a story that in some sense cannot be told.

ASSESSMENTS FOR *THE THINGS THEY CARRIED*

The Things They Carried Written Exam

✍ *College and Career Readiness Anchor Standards for Reading 6–12*

1. Read closely to determine what the text says explicitly and to make logical inferences from it; cite specific textual evidence when writing or speaking to support conclusions drawn from the text.

2. Determine central ideas or themes of a text and analyze their development; summarize the key supporting details and ideas.

5. Analyze the structure of texts, including how specific sentences, paragraphs, and larger portions of the text (e.g., a section, chapter, scene, or stanza) relate to each other and the whole.

6. Assess how point of view or purpose shapes the content and style of a text.

Student Instructions.

Compose a detailed, extended response (250 to 1,000 words) to three of the following:

1. Discuss the shift in narrative distance in the first two stories and *the effect* of that shift.
2. Discuss the various points of view that O'Brien uses in the stories. What are the effects of these different choices?
3. Discuss O'Brien's use of metafiction and the effect of that choice.
4. Discuss the extent to which we find the narrator of these stories reliable.
5. Discuss the choices O'Brien makes that demonstrate a postmodernist approach to fiction.
6. Discuss O'Brien's blending of the genres of fiction and nonfiction and the effect of this choice.
7. In what ways is O'Brien's approach to conveying "truth" postmodernist, and what is revealed by this approach?
8. Discuss O'Brien's use of repetition in the stories and the effect of that choice.

9. Discuss the purpose of a story, according to O'Brien. How is that purpose revealed in the stories?

The Things They Carried Oral Exam

(For the oral version of the exam, use the same nine questions listed in the written version.)

✍ College and Career Readiness Anchor Standards for Speaking and Listening 6–12

1. Prepare for and participate effectively in a range of conversations and collaborations with diverse partners, building on others' ideas and expressing their own clearly and persuasively.

4. Present information, findings, and supporting evidence such that listeners can follow the line of reasoning and the organization, development, and style are appropriate to task, purpose, and audience.

Format of The Things They Carried Oral Exam

- There will be an outer circle and an inner circle.
- Five students at a time will be randomly called into the inner circle.
- Those students may bring notes and their book into the inner circle.
- The 5 students will randomly draw one of the 8 final prompts.
- The 5 students will have a discussion on their prompt.
- They will be graded on the following:
  - Knowledge and familiarity with the stories.
  - Evidence of preparation and analytical thought.
  - Ability to make comments that drive the discussion *forward* and *build upon* what has already been said.

POSTMODERNISM IN *SLAUGHTERHOUSE FIVE*

As in *The Things They Carried,* Kurt Vonnegut's novel *Slaughterhouse Five* employs postmodern experimentation out of a need to tell a story that otherwise could not be adequately told—a story for which traditional storytelling techniques are inadequate.

In Vonnegut's case, he is attempting to tell the story of the firebombing of Dresden, Germany, in World War II, an event that Vonnegut experienced firsthand. In the novel's first chapter, which itself is an example of metafiction, Vonnegut recounts repeated attempts to write a grand, epic novel (using traditional storytelling techniques) about the bombing.

In each case, his attempts failed, and what eventually emerges is not a novel explicitly about the bombing, but a novel about an optometrist named Billy Pilgrim who spontaneously time travels and is kept in a zoo on an alien spaceship. The story of Billy Pilgrim becomes Vonnegut's answer to how one can tell an untellable story.

Traditional conventions of storytelling (rising action, climax, resolution) fail Vonnegut, and like O'Brien, his fiction rejects those techniques, even revealing the novel's beginning, climax, and resolution (if you can call it that) in the first chapter.

CONCEPTS FOR ANALYSIS IN *SLAUGHTERHOUSE FIVE*

Though by no means a complete list, when considering what *Slaughterhouse Five* demonstrates particularly well, this unit can be used to highlight the following academic language and skills.

Motifs

There are a number of motifs present in *Slaughterhouse Five*, most notably the motif of babies/children. For instance, the subtitle of the text (*The Children's Crusade*) is there to remind the reader of Vonnegut's ultimate problem with war: it is fought by children, who kill other children. This is unnatural. He describes his characters as covered with baby fat. Our images of God consist of baby Jesus from the song "Away in a Manger." He also regularly juxtaposes childlike imagery with soldier imagery to connote the innocence and vulnerability of the soldiers of war. This symbolic juxtaposition informs our understanding of Vonnegut's message.

Ironic Juxtapositions and Incongruous Comparisons

Throughout the text, strange things are juxtaposed. For instance, our author describes himself as having breath that stinks of mustard gas and roses. This is an example of something we see throughout the text: violent, destructive images being juxtaposed with calming, pleasant ones. Further, we have the aforementioned incongruous comparison of children as soldiers. Each of those subgroups has their own strong connotative meanings, and when put together they flummox the mind—which is, of course, the point.

Imagery

Vonnegut's imagery is unparalleled, sometimes able to show us the absurdity of situations (the English soldier dressed as the fairy godmother, for instance) but more often to kick us in the guts—a German soldier is described as looking like the biblical Eve; Billy is an absurd flamingo in his prison camp get-up. The imagery is often a reflection of the emotionally detached voice—we *hear* Vonnegut seeing the world in a barren, objective way. Emotional words are kept to a bare minimum; allowing us to be more nakedly affected by what we do see in the text.

Flashback

Students learn repeatedly over the years what a flashback is, but here is a text that really does the technique justice. Throughout *Slaughterhouse Five*, there are a number of images that cause Billy Pilgrim to circle back through time. Each of these we find are initially introduced in the war, though it takes us far into the book (which moves freely through time) to discover that each of these "triggers" has its genesis in the war itself. Some of these are:

- "somewhere a big dog barked";
- "mustard gas and roses";
- "three musketeers"; and
- "spooning".

The purpose of these repeating flashbacks is to suggest that this untellable story is inescapable—such trauma is omnipresent for those who went through it. It also allows us to see the seemingly cold and unfeeling emotional detachedness in the text ("So it goes," for example) as a coping mechanism.

Metafiction

Examples of metafiction are interspersed throughout the novel, but the experimental technique is most apparent in the novel's first chapter. In chapter 1, Vonnegut levels with his audience and relates that it took him years to figure out how to tell this story. Interestingly, he relays the anecdote of trying to outline the story with his daughter's crayons on the back of a roll of wallpaper, but that too failed.

This opening chapter establishes from the beginning that Vonnegut, like O'Brien, struggled to tell the *emotional* truth of his experiences in war.

Beyond chapter 1, the metafiction runs subtly throughout the text. Vonnegut writes himself into the Dresden scenes very quietly, telling the audience offhandedly that he was there, too. Which he was—something that, as readers, we sometimes forget among talk of Tralfamadorians and the ludicrous Billy Pilgrim. Vonnegut does this to draw attention once again to the idea that this entire text is his attempt to tell the emotional truth of an untellable story.

Surrealism

Surrealism, in which reality is overtaken by the dreamlike, irrational, or illogical, is yet another method Vonnegut employs in an attempt to tell a story that traditional techniques fail to adequately tell. Examples in *Slaughterhouse Five* include time travel and human zoos and movies running backward.

Voice

The biggest take-away for many students after reading *Slaughterhouse Five* is the iconic Vonnegut voice, which is an aggregate of a number of elements, most notably his choices in imagery, diction, and juxtaposition. The most famous (and most often repeated) example of this voice is his refrain, "so it goes," which appears after every single death in the text. No matter who or what dies, whether it be Robert F. Kennedy or a bottle of champagne, death in the text is treated equally by his emotionally detached voice.

Curiously, throughout the text, one comes to realize that the very emotional detachedness of the voice allows the reader to feel the impact of tragedy and loss and bewilderment anew. By stripping life's disappointments of their clichés and looking at them blandly, the audience has a new, more authentic emotional response to the loss we hear of in the book.

For example, in chapter 1, Vonnegut describes a horrific incident but chooses to leave out all emotional diction:

> *This veteran decided to take his car into the basement, and he closed the door and started down, but his wedding ring was caught in all the ornaments. She was hoisted into the air and the floor of the car went down, dropped out from under him, and the top of the car squashed him. So it goes.*
>
> *So I phoned this in, and the woman who was going to cut the stencil asked me, "What did his wife say?"*
>
> *he doesn't know yet," I said. "It just happened."*
>
> *"Call her up and get a statement."*
>
> *"What?"*
>
> *"Tell her you're Captain Finn of the Police Department. Say you have some sad news. Give her the news, and see what she says."*
>
> *So I did. She said about what you would expect her to say. There was a baby. And so on.*

When I got back to the office, the woman writer asked me, just for her own information, what the squashed guy had looked like when he was squashed.
I told her.
"Did it bother you?" she said. She was eating a Three Musketeers Candy bar.
"Heck no, Nancy," I said. "I've seen lots worse than that in the war."

Phrases such as, "There was a baby" or "and so on" are so understated and emotionally detached that their effect is much greater. Lines such as these land with a kerplunk on the page. You didn't see them coming, and despite the detached voice, they are heartbreaking.

Activity—Creating Voice through Purposeful Diction

In order to practice recognizing what makes a writer's voice unique, provide opportunities to tell a well-known story and have it become appealing and new *despite* its familiar plot. This is excellent hands-on practice with slippery, abstract postmodern techniques. By using fairytales as the "plot," students can begin to separate *what* happens (plot) from *how* it is composed (voice). What follows is a retelling of "The Three Little Pigs" we created for the purpose of this lesson.

"THE THREE LITTLE PIGS"

This is a story about pigs. Three pigs, to be exact. Exactly three pigs and all three pigs are little. Not that they're baby pigs. They're just little pigs. In fact, they're normal size pigs. We are calling them little pigs as we are viewing them from a human perspective, and pigs are littler than humans. From a pig perspective, they're just normal pigs.

That isn't true. These aren't normal pigs. Normal pigs are born and raised in pig farms and spend their entire lives in small corrals or piled onto trucks. Every now and then a normal pig spends some time in some kid's backyard before being taken to some county fair somewhere but the end result is always the same: normal pigs go to slaughterhouses, which are now called processing plants because that sounds less gruesome where normal pigs are killed and cut up and sent to grocery stores.

These little pigs are not those kinds of pigs. These are the kinds of pigs that are often featured in storybooks or cartoons. These are the kinds of pigs that do human things, such as wear clothes and speak English and build houses.

Speaking of building houses, what happens in this story is that each pig builds a house, which in and of itself is not so interesting. What makes a story interesting, as we all know, is conflict, and as we also know conflict is created by some sort of antagonist, which can take on many forms, such as a monster or self-doubt or a tornado.

In this story, the antagonist takes the form of a Big Bad . . . , etc.

Student Instruction

Step One: After reading the (incomplete) story aloud, instruct students to get into pairs and annotate this retelling of *The Three Little Pigs* for choices in diction, imagery, repetition, and so on, that aid in creating the voice—the unique "sound" of the writing. The teacher can then facilitate a discussion as a whole group about how this voice was created.

Step Two: Students individually retell their own fairy tale, keeping the plot but adding in voice. The challenge will be not getting Vonnegut impersonators. That may take time. But even something that sounds a lot like Vonnegut will teach them how to make choices that move away from straight narrative and toward aesthetic exploration.

Step Three: Students write a one-to-two-page analysis of their retold fairytales discussing how they created voice in their own piece. This forces students to reflect on the effectiveness of their choices.

Taking it Further

As an extra step, you can have students swap their retellings of the story the next day, and annotate their peer's stylistic choices. This will provide more exposure to voice and style, while also providing another opportunity for annotating text and applying the academic language they've been acquiring.

RECOGNIZING AND APPRECIATING SURREALISM

Teaching postmodernism and its major characteristics—absurdism and surrealism—can be a bit abstract for lots of students. The key is finding the right passages with which to teach the concept. For *Slaughterhouse Five*, an excellent example is found in chapter 4 when Billy Pilgrim is up late at night watching a movie about the heroes of World War II.

> *Seen backwards by Billy, the story went like this:*
>
> *American planes, full of holes and wounded men and corpses took off backwards from an airfield in England. Over France, a few German fighter planes flew at them backwards, sucked bullets and shell fragments from some of the planes and crewmen. They did the same for wrecked American bombers on the ground, and those planes flew up backwards to join the formation.*

The formation flew backwards over a German city that was in flames. The bombers opened their bomb bay doors, exerted a miraculous magnetism which shrunk the fires, gathered them into cylindrical steel containers, and lifted the containers into the bellies of the planes. The containers were stored neatly in racks. The Germans below had miraculous devices of their own, which were long steel tubes. They used them to suck more fragments from the crewmen and planes. But there were still a few wounded Americans, though and some of the bombers were in bad repair. Over France, though, German fighters came up again, made everything and everybody as good as new.

When the bomber got back to their base, the steel cylinders were taken from the racks and shipped back to the United States of America, where factories were operating night and day, dismantling the cylinders, separating the dangerous contents into minerals. Touchingly, it was mainly women who did this work. The minerals were then shipped to specialists in remote areas. It was their business to put them into the ground, to hide them cleverly, so they would never hurt anybody again.

The American fliers turned in their uniforms, became high school kids. And Hitler turned into a baby, Billy Pilgrim supposed. That wasn't in the movie. Billy was extrapolating. Everybody turned into a baby, and all humanity, without exception, conspired biologically to produce two perfect people named Adam and Eve, he supposed.

By employing the dreamlike reality of surrealism, Vonnegut has given his readers much to notice:

- The motif of babies is present, particularly the juxtaposition of soldiers to babies. This also demonstrates Vonnegut's use of incongruous comparisons for symbolic effect.
- The theme of questioning the usefulness of war is indicated.
- The Tralfamadorian concept of time is seen, which underscores both emotional detachedness and psychotic breaks in the text.
- The absurdity of seeing the war move backward allows us to understand an emotional truth: war causes destruction and loss of innocence—people should aim to protect each other, not destroy each other.

This passage shows students the importance (or the "so what?") of surrealism: it allows for an emotional truth to register more authentically than telling a realistic narrative ever could.

Once students have an understanding of what surrealism, absurdism, and metafiction are, they can try their own hand at finding quality examples from the text that demonstrate all of the above and work together to create the unique Vonnegut voice.

Activity—Examining the Voice in Vonnegut

Student Instructions

In small groups, find three passages throughout the text of *Slaughterhouse Five* that demonstrate a strong literary voice. Passages are first come, first served, so once you've decided on your three, make sure they are still available from your teacher.

1. Print copies of each passage for disbursement to the class.
2. As a group, annotate each passage and come to an agreement about what you are seeing that creates distinct voice and style. Is it imagery? Connotation? Incongruous comparisons? Pacing? Apply all terms studied so far to what you see.
3. In a jigsaw activity, create new groups with one representative (along with their three passages) from each original group. Students will share their passages and explain how voice and style has been accomplished in that particular passage.

These passages can then be used in a final exam as passages to annotate and write a close-read response for. The activity will create a bank of twelve to eighteen passages that students will have chosen, annotated, and discussed. They can use this bank to study for the test, and you need only choose one or two that most exemplify the skills you are most concerned with students mastering.

Notice that the students are in charge of finding appropriate examples. They have the support of a small group initially, but they still must demonstrate familiarity with the text. Also, once again, the teacher in this activity is observing and helping, not leading. The students are leading their learning.

As always, to ensure that activities and tasks in your class are treated with urgency, give them the bare minimum amount of time in class to complete the stages of this activity. You want it done well, but you also want them working from bell to bell. If you overhear someone saying, "We'll just do the rest tomorrow," you've allowed too much time.

ASSESSMENTS FOR *SLAUGHTERHOUSE FIVE*

Short Answer Exam

✍ College and Career Readiness Anchor Standards for Writing 6–12

1. Write arguments to support claims in an analysis of substantive topics or texts, using valid reasoning and relevant and sufficient evidence.

9. Draw evidence from literary and/or informational texts to support analysis, reflection, and research.

Student Instructions

Each of the following should be answered thoroughly and with multiple examples from the text (1–2 pages each).

1. How and why is the motif of babies present in *Slaughterhouse Five*?
2. Identify and examine the purpose of three examples of flashback in *Slaughterhouse Five.*
3. Discuss the importance of the following passage:
   "The guards drew together instinctively, rolled their eyes. They experimented with one expression and then another, said nothing, though their mouths were often open. They looked like a silent film of a barbershop quartet.
   'So long forever,' they might have been singing, 'old fellows and pals; so long forever, old sweethearts and pals—God bless 'em—'"
4. What purpose does Tralfamadorian philosophy serve in the text?
5. What purpose does metafiction serve in the text?

Timed-Writing Exam

✍ College and Career Readiness Anchor Standards for Writing 6–12

1. Write arguments to support claims in an analysis of substantive topics or texts, using valid reasoning and relevant and sufficient evidence.

9. Draw evidence from literary and/or informational texts to support analysis, reflection, and research.

In keeping with the goal of having students interact repeatedly with the text in order to move past *what* happens and discover, instead, *why* it happens, consider a timed-writing exam. The following is a list of possible prompts for an open-book timed-writing assessment that will allow you to check for student understanding of the skills presented in the unit. Each of the following prompts will force the students to find relevant, effective evidence, demonstrate their working knowledge of the academic language procured so far in the unit, and write a logically cohesive argument.

Notice how the questions never lead students to a particular passage or moment; rather, the students must interact with the text themselves, independently, to piece together the most effective response. This, too, mirrors the written prompts for the Common Core examinations and helps build student confidence with such types of assessments.

Timed-Writing Prompts

1. What do incongruous comparisons like "mustard gas and roses" signal to the audience about the state of mind of the narrator?
2. Why do phrases like "three musketeers" and "somewhere a big dog barked" send Billy Pilgrim traveling through time? What other phrases trigger Billy to move through time in the text. Why?
3. Is this an antiwar text? Why/why not?
4. How does the end of the novel reinforce major themes in the text?

Group Presentation

✍ College and Career Readiness Anchor Standards for Speaking and Listening 6–12

1. Prepare for and participate effectively in a range of conversations and collaborations with diverse partners, building on others' ideas and expressing their own clearly and persuasively.

4. Present information, findings, and supporting evidence such that listeners can follow the line of reasoning and the organization, development, and style are appropriate to task, purpose, and audience.

5. Make strategic use of digital media and visual displays of data to express information and enhance understanding of presentations.

What follows is an option for a group project that combines reading, writing, and listening and speaking standards.

Possible Topics

1. Themes in *Slaughterhouse Five*
2. Psychotic breaks
3. Emotional detachedness
4. Kerplunks and Whammies (These are words or phrases in the text that have a highly dramatic effect, but are presented totally without drama—for instance, when Vonnegut tells the audience he, too, was with Billy Pilgrim in Dresden, or the barbershop quartet scene.)
5. Dresden bombing
6. Cultural influence of *Slaughterhouse Five*
7. Motif of babies
8. Surrealism
9. Incongruous comparisons
10. The importance of Tralfamadorians to the purpose of the text
11. Effect of metafiction

Student Instructions

- Pick one of the above to master.
- Include a works-cited page using MLA formatting.
- Include evidence from a variety of chapters.
- Create a student-made art piece, with no white space, that augments your project—it does not need to be literal, but it must be powerful.
- Create a 7–10 minute lesson on your subject for the class.
- Create a brief assessment for the class (which will be graded!) that is based on your lesson.

Things to think about:

- I can mute any group member at any time, so every group member needs to know everything.
- We will use a portion of your student-created assessment on the final unit test.
- Research must be academic in nature and use appropriate, academic sources.

This assignment works well because it covers so much ground. The list above provides a variety of possibilities, so students can choose something that really interests them. It insists on research and citation skills, so if that is something that needs teaching or reteaching, you can spend one to two days of this unit focused on that. Additionally, this could be an ideal place to teach evaluating the validity of research sources.

Students are once again *independently* interacting for a second time with the text. They haven't just read the chapters, they are now revisiting the chapters and gathering the best, most influential evidence. This creates a depth of applied knowledge that students will benefit from. It demands cooperation from a group, rehearsing a quality presentation, and accountability from every student in the room.

SUMMARY

This chapter has demonstrated how we must move students away from the assumption that reading is for plot. Sometimes, the subtleties of the text tell us a great deal about the purpose of the text. *Slaughterhouse Five* and *The Things They Carried* move in and out of time and have no clear resolution, but what they do have are distinct choices that point to the thesis of the texts: there's nothing to be said about human atrocities like genocides or war—no words can sufficiently tell that story. Instead, we have surrealistic time travel and moral ambiguity as our answer for such devastation.

This unit allows students to interact constantly with the texts, investigating the details of craft that create voice. By studying texts that break the "rules," students realize that writing is not always formulaic, and in their own writing there is the opportunity to try something totally new—to create and cultivate a unique voice.

Chapter Eight

Toni Morrison's *Beloved*

Recognizing and Evaluating Theme and Purpose in a Complex Text

UNIT QUESTION: TO WHOM DO YOU BELONG?

INTRODUCTION

This chapter will discuss how to create a dynamic, quick-paced reading list for your students' year, as well as demonstrate how choosing challenging literature can be extremely rewarding for students of all abilities. By showcasing a unit revolving around Toni Morrison's *Beloved,* we see how introducing students to texts with more abstract literary techniques (magical realism, circumlocution, surrealism) is a way to increase the rigor of the curriculum, while simultaneously increasing the active involvement between the student and the text.

This chapter will also demonstrate how to authentically teach the concept of theme. This particular term is always on tests, yet is rarely mastered. By using a complex text to track the development of theme over the course of a unit, students will come to understand that themes in literature are often implicit and subtle. Through a series of discussions, Socratic seminars, and close-read exercises, students will see how Morrison uses complex narrative structure to convey themes in the text.

COMMON CORE STANDARDS ADDRESSED

✍ College and Career Readiness Anchor Standards For Reading 6–12

2. Determine central ideas or themes of a text and analyze their development; summarize the key supporting details and ideas.

3. Analyze how and why individuals, events, and ideas develop and interact over the course of the text.

6. Assess how point of view or purpose shapes the content and style of a text.

9. Analyze how two or more texts address similar themes or topics in order to build knowledge or to compare the approaches the authors take.

CHOOSING THE RIGHT READING SYLLABUS

When considering what texts to teach at the high school level, one should try to create a booklist that is varied in terms of genre, literary period, and authors. Too often, high school students in America read one, maybe two novels a year. Typically, these novels are pre–World War II, and often they are written by white men. Therefore, a student may only be exposed to four to eight texts throughout their entire high school career, one-third of which will be Shakespeare, the other two-thirds consisting of a very small pool of authors. If this is the case, we shouldn't be too surprised that we aren't graduating voracious readers.

Instead, take a close look at what your district's approved book list is, and see if there is enough variety on your syllabus. Look for ways to incorporate different literary styles and genres, and see if you can create a syllabus that exposes students to a wide range of possibilities of what literature can do.

The truth is, few of us are interested in everything, and though poetry may work for some, drama may work better for others. When we limit our reading lists so severely, many students begin assuming they don't like reading, when the truth is what all readers know: they don't like what they are being *forced* to read. It's not the same thing as disliking reading at all.

For instance, a sample booklist from the past looks like this:

Summer: *Oedipus Rex* and *The Kite Runner*
Fall: *One Flew Over the Cuckoo's Nest*
Winter: *Beloved*
Spring: Walt Whitman's poetry and *Hamlet*

Six texts, a woman author (something seen far too rarely on high school syllabi), poetry, texts ranging from ancient Greek tragedy to twenty-first century novel—realism, drama, postmodernism, and poetry all included.

Twain and Hawthorne are important authors, and we don't wish to diminish what they can offer students, but it does not follow that there can only be a handful of authors studied all across America within the four years of the typical high school experience, and we should certainly all be able to agree that we need more women and more ethnicities included within these lists.

Creating a list that provides different voices, styles, and genres should *never* mean, however, that we include substandard literature on our syllabi. Remember, the syllabus should reflect important, iconic texts that are the best fit for the skill(s) your unit is based on.

This brings us to including texts that are incredibly challenging, but that have the potential to be game changers for our students. A unit of study on Toni Morrison's *Beloved* works because it is an absolute work of art, is incredibly challenging, opens up a plethora of cross-curricular possibilities, will allow the teacher to build in a significant amount of nonfiction texts that dovetail logically with the unit of study, and showcases many wonderful things in literature American high school students rarely encounter: magical realism, surrealism, circumlocution as the narrative, and postmodern voice. It is also written by a woman, and a woman of color, two demographics too rarely seen on high school reading lists.

Beyond this, though the narrative style blends music, poetry, and prose and is oftentimes difficult to follow as it moves in and out of different character's minds, it also deals with issues that every student has an opinion on: mothers. Everyone has one.

POSSIBLE LECTURES AND DISCUSSIONS FOR *BELOVED* UNIT OF STUDY

What follows is a list of topics for the teacher to cover over the course of the unit. The italicized words demonstrate the skill associated with each topic. All topics should be related back to the question of deciphering and discussing theme within a text. This unit of study will cover the following (potentially new or unmastered) material:

Theme

To discover and examine the theme in a text, a reader must look for what the author seems to want their audience to understand upon reaching its conclusion. Not necessarily a moral or a lesson, a theme can be something abstract and indecisive. The older our students become, the more literary texts (and history and art class and science, etc.) will show them that what we are supposed to "get" by the end is often slippery and may have many sides to it. Morrison uses *Beloved* to propose a surprisingly uncomfortable theme to the audience: What if our mothers are wrong? What if our mothers need more in their lives than just being our mothers?

Throughout the study of the text, have students focus on precise moments where Morrison is clearly developing this theme for the audience. Make students pinpoint exact diction that supports the creation of the theme throughout the entire text. What follows are some helpful questions to keep in mind for you and your students.

- How does Morrison develop theme through her shifting narrative voice?
- What are we, the audience, to understand after reading *Beloved*?

Inference

Close-reading practice will help build mastery of this skill, but basically we want students to understand without being explicitly told. *Beloved* is a perfect text with which to practice inference because it relies so heavily on the reader understanding all that is never directly said. No one ever tells us what or who Beloved is. No one ever tells us what the "hot thing" is. Sethe describes the beauty of the trees on Sweet Home plantation and briefly, in passing, mentions there are dead men hanging from them.

Much of the text depends on inference because of its importance to our understanding of Sethe and the trauma of slavery in America. Many of the characters in the story refuse to directly tell what they have seen and done because they simply can't look back. However, Morrison suggests that even chronic avoidance of such trauma is problematic, because Sethe has her "rememories" to contend with; those moments so terrible that they play like a loop in her mind.

The audience would not understand the significance of psychological scarring or the circumlocution used throughout the text if they weren't first able to infer what Sethe and Morrison are leaving off the page.

What follows are some guiding questions for students about inference and its purpose in the text:

- Morrison uses subtleties, circumlocution, and total avoidance of certain subjects/names/occurrences in the text. Why?
- Intercalary chapters (chapters that do not directly support the plot of the larger text, yet are clearly symbolically important—Steinbeck uses the same narrative technique in *The Grapes of Wrath*, for instance) within the text leave the chronological narrative of Sethe and her family and move in and out of time and place. What do these intercalary chapters allow us to infer about Morrison's ultimate purpose with the text?

Narrative Style and Why It Matters

Morrison is renowned for the musicality and power of her writing. At times, *Beloved* reads like a lyrical poem, at others it breaks rules of grammar and syntax to create new meaning. The following are some specific skills students will need to learn to appreciate and recognize within the text.

Circumlocution

Circumlocution is a narrative device that suggests a deliberate attempt to avoid a subject. The narrative structure of *Beloved* relies heavily on this technique to suggest the psychological scarring inflicted on the characters by the brutality of slavery. For instance, when Paul D returns after years away and discovers how and why Sethe ultimately ran away from Sweet Home plantation, he keeps pressing her to discuss how she was beaten and abused, but she will only concede that "they took her milk." This obvious avoidance of the subject becomes a coping mechanism for Sethe and other characters in the text. They talk, think, dream *around* what has happened to them. It is up to the reader to infer what is being avoided in moments of circumlocution

Switching Perspectives

Morrison switches from first-person point of view to third-person omniscient fluidly throughout the text, in addition to fluidly shifting the first-person point of view from character to character. One effect of this choice is to create a depth of understanding about the cast of characters, but more importantly, it underlines Morrison's goal of the text: to give voice to the sixty million or more people who died within the institution of slavery. In short, by shifting points of view throughout the story, she avoids making this a book about Sethe and instead makes it a story about the "ghost" of slavery in America.

Imagery

Imagery is used in the text to demonstrate motifs, connotation, and symbols. Most importantly, there is an abundance of mother imagery within the text. There is a focus on what makes a person a mother—a biological birth, or a bond between child and mother? Contrary images of motherhood are rampant in the text, and Sethe especially remembers details that tie her to her role as a mother.

- Sethe repeats over and over again, "They took my milk" when discussing the abuse she suffered from Schoolteacher's nephews. Her anger and disgust is never focused on what she endured but on how her abuse affected her ability to nurse her child.

- Sethe's mother's brand was imprinted on her breast. This choice of image suggests the problem of possession posed in the text. The slave owner's brand being placed over the breast suggests that the owner has the right to allow or prevent her from nursing her child. This is unnatural, and underscores the motif of slavery perverting the natural, familial bond.

Nature imagery and symbolism within the text is used to create meaning for the audience. Particular instances of nature imagery to track are the following:

- the chokecherry tree;
- the Ohio River;
- the forest that springs up between Sethe and Paul D.

Paradox

- Sweet Home plantation is described as physically beautiful. Both Paul D and Sethe remember the beauty and comfort of the trees. However, the name is problematic, as we see in flashback the horrors endured there.
- Sethe claims in the climax of the text, when she attempts to kill all of her children, that she must do so to make sure they are safe from the hell of slavery. However, how can murder be understood as a safety measure?

CENTRAL THEMES

Theme One "Anything coming back to life hurts."

This quote is an example of the major theme of the text: that the novel *Beloved* is intended to begin addressing how slavery has become America's ghost story—the more we avoid dealing with the race issues in America, the more they fester and demand attention. Students could trace how this theme is developed both physically (Beloved being resurrected) and metaphorically for Sethe and her community within the text. What follows is a short list of subjects within the book that suggest this theme:

- Paul D and his tobacco tin;
- Sethe and her "rememories"; and
- Beloved's resurrection.

Theme Two: The problem with the concept of possession.

Sethe justifies her choice of attempting to murder her children because she, as their mother, had the right to decide what was best for them. This choice, of course, dismisses the autonomy of young children from their mother. Sethe argues that her children are her "best thing," an extension of who she is. Students will tend to be comfortable with this premise themselves; we are used to the idea of a sacrificial, devoted mother. However, *Beloved* poses the other side of this archetype: what happens to anyone, despite age or relation, whose identity is dependent on their relationship with someone else? It's a slippery slope.

The text also uses this theme to discuss how slavery has perverted the familial bond of those enslaved. Mothers aren't allowed to be mothers because they are needed in the field—they don't raise their own children. Children can be bought and sold without any concern for the familial unit. Of course, this was purposeful to prevent strong bonds between slaves. In this text, Morrison explores how the sickness of such practices may affect a single family once they have escaped to freedom. Sethe and Schoolteacher both assert their right to "own" Sethe's children; this leads to crawling-already? baby's death. Other examples of this from the text are as follows:

- Beloved ends up possessing Sethe leech-like.
- Paul D says you should never love anything too much, or it will possess you.
- Motherhood within the institution of slavery confuses who has what claim to children.

Activity—Tracking and Discussing Theme

✍ College and Career Readiness Anchor Standards for Writing 6–12

1. Write arguments to support claims in an analysis of substantive topics or texts, using valid reasoning and relevant and sufficient evidence.

A novel like *Beloved* does an excellent job of establishing themes from a multitude of perspectives. Because the novel moves in and out of space, time, and different characters' narration, each theme is established from a multitude of fronts, but never with a heavy hand. This allows students to practice recognizing implicit details and making thematic inferences about them.

This unit works for theme because of its complexity. What does Morrison want us to understand by the end of the novel? How do you know? Some possible themes to track are:

1. the importance of acknowledging one's past;
2. the importance of maintaining one's own voice;
3. motherhood/perversion of the familial bond through slavery;

4. storytelling and its power;
5. slavery as America's ghost story; and
6. the problem with the concept of possession—spiritually, physically, economically, and within one's own family.

Provide a packet of excerpts from the novel. For an in-class exercise or a take-home writing assignment, have students choose one passage and write a short paper about how that excerpt demonstrates one of the above themes. Students will have to show understanding of theme, be able to do a close read of a single passage, and use the "little stuff" like diction, imagery, and so on, to discuss the author's purpose within the passage to demonstrate theme.

Figure 8.1 is a student example of an annotated passage. This chosen passage from the beginning of *Beloved* begins to demonstrate the theme of the mother bond.

By interacting with the text thoroughly through annotations, the student is prepared to discuss how an author's choice creates themes to be understood by the audience.

MANIPULATING DICTION

Morrison's manipulation of *diction* creates new, grammatically incorrect yet powerful *connotations* in the text. Throughout *Beloved*, Morrison creates new diction that is far more impactful than if she had kept to traditional, proper syntax. For instance, to demonstrate both circumlocution and psychological scarring, Morrison tells the audience early on that Sethe has her "rememories" with her always. The addition of the prefix "re" shows the audience that there are some specific memories that are constantly with Sethe. The word "rememories" allows the audience to appreciate the degree of her preoccupation with the past and its haunting effect on her. Examples of Morrison manipulating traditional diction from the text are as follows:

- rememories;
- Baby Suggs—Holy;
- crawling-already? baby;
- confusion/lack of punctuation in intercalary chapters.

MAGICAL REALISM

Magical realism asserts that the fantastic can and does exist in the fictional world. That is, things that are logically impossible (a girl with memories a

"No more powerful than the way I loved her," Sethe answered and there it was again. The welcoming cool of unchiseled headstones; the one she selected to lean against on tiptoe, her knees wide open as any grave. Pink as a fingernail it was, and sprinkled with glittering chips. Ten minutes, he said. You got ten minutes I'll do it for free.

Ten minutes for seven letters. With another ten could she gave gotten "Dearly" too? She had not thought to ask him and it bothered her still that it might have been possible—that for twenty minutes, a half hour, say, she could have had the whole thing, every word she heard the preacher say at the funeral (and all there was to say, surely) engraved on her baby's headstone: Dearly Beloved. But what she got, settled for, was the one word that mattered. She thought it would be enough, rutting among the headstones with the engraver, his young son looking on, the anger in his face so old; the appetite in it quite new. That should certainly be enough. Enough to answer one more preacher, one more abolitionist and a town full of disgust.

Counting on the stillness of her own soul, she had forgotten the other one: the soul of her baby girl. Who would have thought that a little old baby could harbor so much rage? Rutting among the stones under the eyes of the engraver's son was not enough. Not only did she have to live out her years in a house palsied by the baby's fury at having its throat cut, but those ten minutes she spent pressed up against dawn-colored stone studded with star chips, her knees wide open as the grave, were longer than life, more alive, more pulsating than the baby blood that soaked her fingers like oil.

"We could move," she suggested once to her mother-in-law

Figure 8.1.

hundred years old, for instance) such as walking out of the water and landing at 124 Bluestone Road could happen. Morrison uses magical realism as a vehicle to demonstrate the ghostliness of this American ghost story. What follows are some examples wherein Morrison relies on magical realism to make the fantastic events of her novel seem believable:

- Beloved as a character;
- moving through space and time and remaining interconnected;
- Beloved remembering slave passage;
- Beloved rising from the water;
- "a hot thing."

CROSS-CURRICULAR POSSIBILITIES

✍ Common Core College and Career Readiness Anchor Standards for Writing

8. Gather relevant information from multiple print and digital sources, assess the credibility and accuracy of each source, and integrate the information while avoiding plagiarism.

9. Draw evidence from literary and/or informational texts to support analysis, reflection, and research.

Ideally, your school site has a concrete plan in place to ensure that units throughout all grade levels are regularly quality, cross-curricular units. What makes a cross-curricular unit a success will be covered in chapter 9, but in short, teachers need to ensure that what students are studying in English class will immediately matter in their history class, perhaps, and vice versa. Learning ceases to be in the bubble of one particular classroom.

A unit on *Beloved* would be ideal for a quality cross-curricular unit of study. The most natural fit for this unit seems to be a crossover between English and History; however, there may be a Math possibility as well.

Common Core Anchor Standards for ELA repeatedly emphasize the importance of research, as well as the student's ability to navigate between informational texts, literature, and their own analysis and reflection. This unit provides a wonderful opportunity to do meaningful research that can be immediately, directly, applied to the text, as well as a natural time to teach (or check for mastery) student understanding of proper citations, research, and plagiarism.

What follows is a list of possibilities for (ideally) a cross-curricular unit of study, or at least a place to incorporate quality informational texts to pair with Morrison's literature:

- crossover with civil war legislation (the Fugitive Slave Act, the Dred Scott decision, and the underground railroad to name only a few);
- slave narrative nonfiction connections (Provide excerpts from *The Life of a Slave Girl* or Fredrick Douglass's autobiography to compare and contrast to Morrison's *Beloved*.);
- informational text crossover possibilities:
    1. Research Morrison's claim of the "sixty million or more."
    2. Why are there so few slave narratives or accounts from slaves who lived both pre and post Civil War?
    3. Research Margaret Garner and similar cases.
    4. Research the reality of the slave ship passage.
    5. Research the international slave trade.
    6. Why was Sethe so valuable? How was value determined?
    7. Lost voices—why weren't slaves allowed to read and write? How did this affect our understanding of slavery?
    8. Why can't we be sure of the 60 million number Morrison cites in the dedication?
    9. How many people were slave ships designed to hold? How many typically arrived?
    10. Why weren't slaves allowed to read or write?

Common Core assessments will ask students to work with unfamiliar informational texts in which students will have to make logical assertions, understand data and statistics, appreciate author's voice, purpose, and intended audience, and more. Because Common Core dictates that all tested subjects will be moving toward a student's original, written responses, all subjects will have to begin providing examples of informational texts and letting students practice their assessments.

Though English teachers should protect the literature on their syllabus, we should also be looking for engaging informational texts and research possibilities for students so that they can practice applying research and nonfiction to the fiction it connects with.

For instance, Morrison says that she wrote *Beloved* to give voice to the "sixty million or more" who lost their lives in slavery and the international slave trade. The novel is a work of imagination necessitated by all those millions who lost their voice. This statistic is a perfect, important piece of information for students to gain exposure to nonfiction texts that relate to the number.

If the pacing aligns across the curriculum, consider what a text like this could do when paired up with a history classroom. Students could study an incredible example of literature, and also gain a thorough, authentic understanding of Civil War–era legislation, the significance of storytelling on the national memory, and an appreciation of the economic, political, and personal ramifications of the slave trade. It could be an amazingly powerful unit.

Taking it Further

If you wanted to tailor this unit to pairing fiction with nonfiction and research, questions such as these could be the basis of a group research assignment that culminated in an oral presentation linking the researching standards to Common Core listening and speaking standards.

Teachers could also use this opportunity to have students compose a research paper—either individually or as a group. This is another opportunity for students to study the symbiotic nature between the nonfiction and fiction texts, as well a full-process paper opportunity.

ADDITIONAL ACTIVITIES

The Close Read

✍ College and Career Readiness Anchor Standards for Writing 6–12

4. Produce clear and coherent writing in which the development, organization, and style are appropriate to task, purpose, and audience.

Have students perform a close read of the first two sentences of the book: "124 was spiteful. Full of baby's venom."

Give them a short amount of time to do this so that there is urgency in their writing.

If this close reading exercise were done at the beginning of the unit, students should see how Morrison is establishing mood and foreshadowing future events. If done again, after students have read more of the text, the close read should discuss *why* she *had* to begin her book that way—as always, close reads should address the ever-important question: *So what?*

Figure 8.2 is a student example of a close read of the first two sentences of the novel. Notice how the student incorporates both knowledge of the text, as well as applies their learned literary terminology to their discussion of the author's choices.

"124 was Spiteful. Full of a baby's venom."

The fact that the house (124) is ~~used~~ introduced more as a character rather than a building shows the personification of the house for those in the story. ~~Th~~ A house is something lived in by the main characters, yet it is never strictly identified as a house, and the diction of home is never used. By stating 124 instead of naming the building the house and its "character" are distanced from the family living there. ~~and similar~~ There is no loving connotation given by the house number which could in itself ~~coul~~ subtextually show that there is no love for the building the family lives in. The ~~na~~ diction of the name 124 is in itself strange. The 3 is ommitted ~~in the~~ because of the ~~death~~ murder of Sethe's third child by her own hand. This ommission can be viewed as a feeling of guilt or remorse, ~~w~~ as if ~~running from~~ not talking about the child will put her out of Sethe's memory forever.

Yet ~~&~~ the child cannot be forgotten. The diction in the personification of the house connotes that the house itself is hateful, and uncaring. This could stem from the "baby's venom." The juxtaposition of "baby's venom" connotes an unnatural ~~feeling~~ mood in the house, as the two things being juxtaposed are not similar. The connotation of "baby" is pure, helpless, soft, innocent, and when paired with "venom" which connotes death, danger and poision creates a very unnatural child.

The diction of "a" is important because it denotes that there is one child and it is a specific child that has venom. This foreshadows that something must happen that is bad to the child to change it from being a normal baby into something unnatural.

The diction of "full" ~~in the~~ connotes that ~~the~~ 124 is overflowing with a baby's venom" ~~and~~ It suggests that no more venom can be put in the house.

Figure 8.2.

The Socratic Seminar

✍ College and Career Readiness Anchor Standards for Speaking and Listening 6–12

1. Prepare for and participate effectively in a range of conversations and collaborations with diverse partners, building on others' ideas and expressing their own clearly and persuasively.

Assign students a topic to prepare. The topic must be open-ended and complex enough that there is a variety of examples to pull from to support both sides of the argument. For instance, the statement "*We, the audience, should condone the killing of crawling-already? baby.*"

Grade student participation in the Socratic seminar with particular attention to:

- their quality of evidence;
- their quantity of evidence;
- how their contributions pushed the conversation forward.

After the Socratic seminar has taken place, have students write a one-page reflection about the most compelling arguments they heard. What evidence compelled them to reevaluate their stance? What was important but never mentioned?

The Weekly Essay

✍ College and Career Readiness Anchor Standards for Writing 6–12

1. Write arguments to support claims in an analysis of substantive topics or texts, using valid reasoning and relevant and sufficient evidence.

5. Develop and strengthen writing as needed by planning, revising, editing, rewriting, or trying a new approach.

Beloved can be a very difficult text to read, and students may have to read sections multiple times to understand what is happening in the story. In order to keep momentum in the room and engagement in the rather long text, consider embracing the weekly essay.

Remember in the writing chapter when we told you that if you are reading everything your students are writing, they aren't writing enough? Well, this may be an excellent example of that. This may be a unit in which the instructor should use the strategies displayed in that chapter in order to keep students writing often, but to keep the grading load reasonable for the instructors as well.

Design a list of essay prompts for your students that particularly address different parts of the novel. This will force students to revisit small chunks of the text and create original, analytical pieces of writing that utilize appropriate textual evidence that supports their thesis.

Possible Weekly Essay Topics for Beloved

1. Discuss breast imagery in the text.
2. How is the novel an example of a bildungsroman for Denver?
3. How does Morrison use imagery to create voice in *Beloved*?
4. Discuss examples of circumlocution or avoidance to demonstrate psychological scarring.
5. Do you blame Sethe for what she does to her children? Why or why not?
6. Discuss the importance of naming (or the refusal to name) within the text.
7. Discuss the difference in tone between *Beloved* and slave narratives of the time. How do you account for this? What does the difference in tone signify?

The list can be added to or subtracted from. However, let's note a few key things:

- Every prompt can and should relate back to the question of theme. Students will use a variety of methods to examine and discuss the development of theme within a text and discuss that theme using a variety of literary terms and skills.
- Every prompt will require specific references to the text—perhaps even negotiating between texts in the slave narrative example. The prompts are specific enough that students must repeatedly and actively engage in the text, thereby creating comfort and familiarity with even a difficult text.
- All topics are analytical in nature. This allows students to continue their practice of finding *their* voice and *their* opinions about the literature.
- Finally, notice that *what* happens is never the end of the question. Each question moves past mere comprehension and forces students to create "why/how" arguments about authorial choice. An English class should not be about what happens but, rather, only an examination of how and why the art was created and whether or not it is effectual in its aims.

The length of the essay should be determined by your grade level and the students' abilities, however don't shy away from a extended length paper (three to five pages, for example) for each. Remember, by keeping the rigor high, the students are constantly reaching. That should be a key goal as educators—avoiding student complacency and keeping them pushing for the next level of achievement.

By the end of the unit, students will have written at least five short essays, one or two more formal process papers, possibly a research paper linking their nonfiction texts to the novel, and an in-class exam of the teacher's own design. This means students will have created approximately twenty-five pages of analytical, written response to one text. The amount of quality practice embedded in a unit such as this will undoubtedly increase a student's comfort level with the written Common Core exams.

The volume of work produced here provides students with ample opportunity to practice writing. Their theses will be stronger and their evidence gathering more persuasive, and their confidence in applying literary skills and terminology to outside material will increase.

SUMMARY

Consider what a unit like this does in regard to preparation for the end-of-year Common Core assessments. Students of varying ability will have spent ten or so weeks engaging in a highly difficult and demanding text. They will have felt a personal connection to the text via the initial essential question. They will have created an astounding amount of original written analysis about that work.

They will also have practiced the skills of summarizing, incorporating textual evidence, tracking theme through a text, and researching and evaluating informational sources, and they will have created an impressive body of original work, all of which allows them to practice creating quality, thoughtful written responses when it comes to the test. They will conclude this unit feeling confident about what theme is, recognizing its slippery nature and prepared to find it in a variety of fiction and nonfiction texts in preparation for their Common Core exams.

No worksheets were used, no bubbles were filled in. They are meeting the story of Sethe, Paul D, and Beloved and connecting to it themselves—and finding they have lots to say. This type of interaction creates learners the way bubbling never can.

Chapter Nine

The Adventures of Huckleberry Finn and Abraham Lincoln

Designing a Cross-Curricular Unit of Study

UNIT QUESTION: HOW DO YOU CHANGE HISTORY WHEN HISTORY IS AGAINST YOU?

INTRODUCTION

This chapter will present an example of a cross-curricular unit of study that uses a classic work of literature as a catalyst for a historical discussion of slavery in the United States. This cross-curricular unit will evaluate Huck Finn's decision to free the runaway slave Jim as a microcosm of Abraham Lincoln's decision to pursue passage of the 13th Amendment in 1865, ending American slavery.

In the case of both Huck and Lincoln, a decision had to be made that ran counter to the desires and expectations of society. Both decisions were high stakes, and in both decisions there was an easier way out. Most importantly, in both cases, the pressures of external forces were overcome to make a decision that had a monumental and lasting impact: in the case of Huck Finn, that impact is local and individual; in the case of Lincoln, it is universal.

COMMON CORE STANDARDS ADDRESSED

✍ College and Career Readiness Anchor Standards for Reading 6–12

1. Read closely to determine what the text says explicitly and to make logical inferences from it; cite specific textual evidence when writing or speaking to support conclusions drawn from the text.

2. Determine central ideas or themes of a text and analyze their development; summarize the key supporting details and ideas.

3. Analyze how and why individuals, events, and ideas develop and interact over the course of a text.

5. Analyze the structure of texts, including how specific sentences, paragraphs, and larger portions of the text (e.g., a section, chapter, scene, or stanza) relate to each other and the whole.

6. Assess how point of view or purpose shapes the content and style of a text.

> 8th Grade: Analyze how differences in the points of view of the characters and the audience or reader (e.g., created through the use of dramatic irony) create such effects as suspense or humor.
>
> 11th to 12th Grade: Analyze a case in which grasping point of view requires distinguishing what is directly stated in a text from what is really meant (e.g., satire, sarcasm, irony, or understatement).

9. Analyze how two or more texts address similar themes or topics in order to build knowledge or to compare the approaches the authors take.

> 11th to 12th Grade: Demonstrate knowledge of eighteenth-, nineteenth- and early-twentieth-century foundational works of American literature, including how two or more texts from the same period treat similar themes or topics.

10. Read and comprehend complex literary and informational texts independently and proficiently.

BEFORE READING: PREPARING FOR THE "N-WORD"

Perhaps the greatest challenge in teaching, or even reading, *The Adventures of Huckleberry Finn* is its use of racially offensive language, specifically the "n-word." How do you justify teaching a text, written by a white man, that uses such a hateful and negatively charged word 219 times?

The least effective approach to this problem is to ignore it. An open and detailed discussion of this unavoidable aspect of the novel is vital and should occur before the class even opens the book.

Activity—Banned Books

A potential way to begin this discussion is to take a look at the history of banned books in the United States. Have students (or groups of students) conduct research on books that have been recently banned by school boards. Students should gather information on what books were banned, from where they were banned, who banned them, and the reason that they were banned.

Students may be surprised to discover that some of their favorite books, such as *The Fault in Our Stars*, have been banned in several school districts throughout the country. This research can be conducted informally or can be the basis for formal group presentations—each group, for example, reporting on a different banned book.

Once the class has conducted this research and has examined examples of banned books, guide the class in a discussion of the following question:

Under what circumstances (if any) should a book be removed from schools and/or libraries?

Encourage students, in the course of this discussion, to defend their responses with specific details and examples. This discussion can then be steered, more specifically, to the use of the "n-word." Ask students the following questions:

- Should a book be banned from schools if it repeatedly uses the "n-word"?
- What conclusions can we make about a book that repeatedly uses the "n-word"?

You may be surprised to find that, even in a middle school setting, students often acknowledge that it is difficult to answer this question out of context—that the intent and purpose of the word's use matters.

Students already familiar with Harper Lee's *To Kill a Mockingbird* may be interested to discover that the novel uses the "n-word" forty-eight times. Should *To Kill a Mockingbird*, therefore, be taught in schools? What "context" would make such frequent use of the word acceptable?

And, turning now to *The Adventures of Huckleberry Finn*, what context makes acceptable the use of the "n-word" 219 times? These are important questions to have and important discussions to let run their course before reading the novel.

Turning the Discussion toward Satire

One goal of this unit is for students to recognize and analyze Twain's use of satire in the novel. Satire is difficult to teach and can be difficult for students to appreciate. It is another "problem" that comes along with teaching this novel, but one that should not be ignored and should be initially addressed before students begin reading.

In 2011, New South Books released a modified version of *The Adventures of Huckleberry Finn*. In their new edition, New South replaced every instance of the "n-word" with the word "slave," their intent being to provide an alternative, less offensive version of the book for use in schools. The following link is to a broadcast on CBS's "60 Minutes" newsmagazine show, discussing this new version: http://www.cbsnews.com/videos/huckleberry-finn-and-the-n-word.

This "alternative version" sparked numerous *satirical* responses that can be shared with students, both to further the discussion of the novel's use of the "n-word" and to provide students with contemporary examples of satire.

One such example is a Kickstarter.com campaign posted by the comedy team Diani and Devine and intended to raise funds for *The Adventures of Huckleberry Finn: Robotic Edition*, which, in a tongue-in-cheek effort to produce a version even less offensive than New South's, replaces every instance of the "n-word" with the word *robot*.

The video that accompanies Diani and Devine's Kickstarter campaign can be found at the following link: https://www.kickstarter.com/projects/dianidevine/replacing-the-n-word-with-robot-in-huck-finn/description.

Students may initially struggle to recognize or define satire, but they are certainly familiar with sarcasm. Young people know sarcasm when they see it (or hear it). It is a tool of their trade, and this video is filled with it. The sarcasm in the video makes it clear that replacing the "n-word" with *robot* is a ridiculous solution, thereby implying that the insertion of *slave* is by extension also ridiculous: both are an attempt to avoid an uncomfortable truth.

Defining Satire and Irony

Satire should be defined for students as the use of *humor* and/or *irony* and/or *exaggeration* to ridicule something (often society or an aspect of society).

There are three types of irony students should be familiar with:

- Verbal Irony: when someone says something but means the opposite (this often takes the form of sarcasm). For example, "Oh, great! It's Monday!"
- Situational Irony: when a situation is the opposite of what is expected or what is appropriate. For example, being run over by an ambulance.
- Dramatic Irony: when the reader or audience knows something that a character doesn't. For example, a character in a scary movie walks into a house, but the audience has already been shown that the killer is in the house. Basically, dramatic irony occurs when the reader/audience is aware that the character is making a mistake, even though the character is not aware.

The *Robotic Edition* video, as an example of satire, uses humor (it is very funny), irony (it is filled with sarcasm—making it funny), and exaggeration (it exaggerates the idea of inserting *slave* to make *Huckleberry Finn* less offensive) to ridicule the New South version of the novel.

An understanding of satire and irony (at least an initial understanding) is vital as students begin to read *The Adventures of Huckleberry Finn*, as they will find its pages filled with it, even prior to the start of chapter 1. Such understanding is also a requirement of the Common Core at both the eighth- and eleventh- to twelfth-grade levels.

✍ *8RL6. Analyze how differences in the points of view of the characters and the audience or reader (e.g., created through the use of dramatic irony) create such effects as suspense or humor.*

11–12RL6. Analyze a case in which grasping point of view requires distinguishing what is directly stated in a text from what is really meant (e.g., satire, sarcasm, irony, or understatement).

The Notice and Front Matter

Chapter 1 of *Huckleberry Finn* is preceded by a "Notice" from the author, which reads as follows:

Notice

> *Persons attempting to find a motive in this narrative will be prosecuted; persons attempting to find a moral in it will be banished; persons attempting to find a plot will be shot.*
>
> *BY ORDER OF THE AUTHOR*
> *Per G.G., CHIEF OF ORDNANCE*

Students should be guided in a "close reading" of this notice, as it reveals some interesting things. A good place to start is simply asking students what the intention of this notice is—what is its purpose? Upon examination, it becomes clear that it is not literal: persons violating this notice will certainly not be prosecuted, shot, or banished—it is a notice that cannot be enforced. So, then, what is its purpose, and what is the effect of such strong, and even outlandish, threats?

Students should recognize that the notice itself is sarcastic—an example of verbal irony—and its implicit intention is to instruct the reader to do exactly what it warns against, most notably to find *the motive* and *the moral*. Students will also notice the misspelling of the word *ordinance*. Published novels have been through the copyediting process, and therefore rarely include misspellings of this kind, especially in the front matter, unless that misspelling is *intentional*. So what is the purpose of this misspelling? What is its effect?

First of all, it is an example of dramatic irony, we the readers being aware of G.G., Chief of Ordnance's mistake, though he is not. The effect of this dramatic irony, much like the verbal irony in the notice's content, is to prompt the reader not to take the notice literally, or seriously.

Twain's notice, therefore, *trains* the reader in how to properly read the novel. As students will discover, Huck is a character that at every turn is shortsighted and makes mistakes, though he is unaware of these mistakes. Critical readers of the novel, however, *are* aware, so that when Huck declares in the novel's climax that he will "go to hell" for the abominable crime of helping Jim to freedom, the reader can see that the true abomination is the *deprivation* of Jim's freedom.

It is also from this stance—a stance of dramatic irony—that Twain intended for us to read Huck's use of the "n-word."

CLOSE READING CHAPTER 1

> *You don't know about me without you have read a book by the name of The Adventures of Tom Sawyer; but that ain't no matter. That book was made by Mr. Mark Twain, and he told the truth, mainly. There was things which he stretched, but mainly he told the truth. That is nothing. I never seen anybody but lied one time or another, without it was Aunt Polly, or the widow, or maybe Mary. Aunt Polly—Tom's Aunt Polly, she is—and Mary, and the Widow Douglas is all told about in that book, which is mostly a true book, with some stretchers, as I said before.*

Perhaps the most significant accomplishment of this opening paragraph in chapter 1 is the distinction made between Huck and Mark Twain. It is made clear from the outset that narrator and author are not one in the same, and if you believe Huck, Twain was merely the man who wrote *The Adventures of Tom Sawyer*, having done so with only a handful of lies, and is not necessarily the author of *The Adventures of Huckleberry Finn.*

A reader, of course, is fully aware that though Huck and Twain indeed are not synonymous, and that the "voice" of Huck is not the author's, it is Twain who supplies Huck with his voice.

The effect of this is simple: the voice narrating the novel is human and not authorial. Huck says it himself: "I never seen anybody what didn't lie one time or another." We, as humans, are all fallible, and despite the omniscience we often assign to an "author," even they cannot escape this fallibility.

Students should be aware that with any novel that is narrated in first person, the reader must question the reliability of that narrator, precisely for the reason that the narrator is a character—a person—and not an authorial presence. This is one of the most important distinctions between first-person and third-person limited points of view.

When Huck goes on to say that "The Widow Douglas took me for her son, and allowed she would sivilize me," the students will once again recognize an intentional misspelling—this time of the word *civilize*—creating another example of dramatic irony.

The concept of Huck being civilized is important to explore more deeply. Remember that in the gap between the years when the novel is set and when it was written and published, the United States was involved in the *Civil* War.

Activity—Defining "Civil"

List the words *civil*, *civilized*, and *civilization* on the board and ask groups of students to define each of the terms in their own words. Feel free to provide the groups with dictionaries, but it is important that they are able to produce a definition in their own words. Encourage the groups to share out their definitions, and guide the class in arriving at an agreed-upon definition for each term.

Use the results of this activity to drive a class discussion centered on the following questions:

- How civilized is our society? (on a scale of 1–10)
- What makes our society civilized?
- What makes our society uncivilized?

Students will return to this conversation after reading the remainder of chapter 1 and assessing the extent to which the society in which Huck lives is civilized. The concept of *civilization* is central to the novel, particularly in contrast to that which is not civilized, which in the following paragraph Huck equates with *freedom*:

> *The Widow Douglas she took me for her son, and allowed she would sivilize me; but it was rough living in the house all the time, considering how dismal regular and decent the widow was in all her ways; and so when I couldn't stand it no longer I lit out. I got into my old rags and my sugar-hogshead again, and was free and satisfied. But Tom Sawyer he hunted me up and said he was going to start a band of robbers, and I might join if I would go back to the widow and be respectable. So I went back.*

It is clear here that Huck, somewhat ironically, associates civilization and regularity and decency and respectability with a negative experience—"rough living"—as opposed to life outside of the civilized world of the Widow, where he feels "free and satisfied."

Huck seems to be in a state of flux, moving in and out of civilization. Students will see this again and again as they read the novel, and they should be on the lookout for this conflict between freedom and civilization. In their history class, students will be able to discuss this conflict as a reflection of the spirit of westward expansion that was prevalent in nineteenth-century America.

Also central to this novel is the concept of freedom, which Huck introduces in the above passage. Both Huck and Jim are seeking freedom throughout the novel, though for each of them, "freedom" means something quite different. For Huck, it is a matter of comfort and satisfaction; for Jim, it is a matter of life and death, and discussions in history class will highlight the brutal realities of slavery that are only implicit in the novel.

Huck's ironic description of the Widow's "civilized" ways is no mistake. Throughout the novel, students will recognize that institutions and individuals that are supposed to be "civilized" are quite the opposite. Students should be reminded that this use of irony to ridicule aspects of society is *satire*.

To fully appreciate such satire, students will need to be familiar with *hypocrisy* and what it means to be a *hypocrite*. An early example comes in chapter 1:

> Pretty soon I wanted to smoke, and asked the widow to let me. But she wouldn't. She said it was a mean practice and wasn't clean, and I must try to not do it any more. That is just the way with some people. They get down on a thing when they don't know nothing about it. Here she was a-bothering about Moses, which was no kin to her, and no use to anybody, being gone, you see, yet finding a power of fault with me for doing a thing that had some good in it. And she took snuff, too; of course that was all right, because she done it herself.

The widow, of course, is hypocritical in her prohibiting Huck from smoking tobacco when she uses snuff tobacco. Another example, also in chapter 1, is the following: "By and by they fetched the niggers in and had prayers, and then everybody was off to bed."

Students should be guided in discussing the significance of this sentence, particularly the significance of the widow and Miss Watson, who are religious, owning slaves, and praying with those slaves at the end of their day of unpaid labor. Students may also comment on the connotations of "fetched." This should also be viewed in the context of the widow's demand that Huck "must help other people, and do everything [he] could for other people, and look out for them all the time."

After reading chapter 1, revisit the earlier questions regarding civilization:

How civilized is the society in which Huck lives? (on a scale of 1–10)
What makes the society civilized?
What makes the society uncivilized?

In history class, these same questions could be applied to the society of which Lincoln was president: to what extent was the United States in the Civil War era civilized?

A point of discussion could be the *Dred Scott* decision of 1858, in which the Supreme Court essentially declared slavery a constitutionally protected institution. In the decision, Chief Justice Roger B. Taney eliminated *all* African Americans—not only slaves—as potential citizens. Despite illustrating a potential lack of civility in Lincoln's society, such an example will also make clear to students just how bleak Jim's situation is.

Students should leave chapter 1 with an understanding of the following:

- the satirical nature of the novel;
- the dramatic irony created by Huck's narration;
- the conflict between freedom and civilization; and
- the hypocrisy of "civilized" society.

GUIDING QUESTIONS

The following questions can be used to guide students' reading of the first half of the novel. These questions can be used for the purposes of informal class discussions but can also be used as essay topics or presentation topics (or both).

Chapters 1–13

- How civilized is the society in which Huck lives?
- How important is superstition to the society in which Huck lives?
- Compare/contrast the characters of Huck Finn and Tom Sawyer.
- How does Twain use various types of irony in this novel? What is the effect of the irony?
- What kind of father figure is Pap?
- How is Huck in a conflict between freedom and civilization?

Chapters 14–21

- In what ways is nature (or elements of nature) important to the novel's plot?
- In what ways is Huck's ability to "think on his feet" important to the novel's plot?

- How could the river function as a *symbol* of freedom (or the possibility of freedom) in the novel? (For both Huck and Jim?)
- Compare/contrast Huck and Jim.
- Is Huck a moral person? In other words, does he have a good sense of what is right and what is wrong?
- How does Huck's journey for freedom compare/contrast to Jim's journey for freedom?
- Nature versus Civilization: How do Huck's experiences on shore compare/contrast with his experiences on the river?

HUCK'S MORALITY

As students reach chapter 16 of the novel, an opportunity presents itself to discuss Huck's morality, and the role of his conscience in his decisions, which will later play a dominant role in the novel's climax.

First of all, students should know the meanings of both *morality* and *conscience.* Similarly to before, allow students to generate their own definitions, based upon their prior knowledge, but ultimately steer students toward the following definitions (or similar definitions):

- morality (n.): a system of ideas of right and wrong behavior;
- conscience (n.): the part of your mind that makes you aware of your actions as being either morally right or wrong.

Activity—Where Does Our Morality Come From?

Once these definitions are established, ask students where their morality, or sense of right and wrong, comes from. Did they *learn* it, or is it just a part of them? If it is learned, from where did they learn it?

Students often begin by claiming that their morality is an inherent part of them, closely tied to their individual nature, but if the discussion delves deeper, students recognize the extent to which their morality is tied to the context that surrounds them—the extent to which it is learned.

Continue by asking students how their morality has changed over the years, or how it is still changing. Exploration of these questions will prepare students to deal with Huck's struggles with his conscience and the evolution of his morality.

This conversation will serve to reinforce the unit question (How do you change history when history is against you?), as both Huck and Lincoln are forced to make a moral decision that is contrary to the agreed-upon morality of their respective societies. (Note: *Huck Finn* was published in 1885 but is set in approximately 1840; the period in which this unit is examining Lincoln is 1862 to 1865.)

Activity—Is Huck a Moral Person?

In turning the discussion to Huck, simply ask the following questions:

- Is Huck a moral person? Why or why not?
- What happens in chapter 13 that helps us better understand Huck's morality? (hint: the incident with the robbers on the wrecked steamboat)
- What happens in chapter 15 that helps us better understand Huck's morality? (hint: it involves Huck and Jim on the raft after the storm)

Examining Huck's "moral" decisions in chapters 13 and 15—not leaving the murderers to die and "humbling" himself to apologize to Jim, respectively—sets the students up for an important moment in chapter 16, in which Huck wrestles with the morality of his involvement in Jim's plan to escape from Miss Watson. Huck's upbringing has trained him to view Jim as Miss Watson's property, and thereby the escape of Jim to be stealing from a poor old woman who never did anything except try to help him.

The thought of betraying Miss Watson in this way makes Huck feel "so mean and so miserable" that he wished he was dead, and his conscience initially leads him to the decision to turn Jim in at the first chance, which relieves the guilt he had felt, but Jim's excitement at believing himself close to freedom, and his declaration of Huck as "de bes' fren' Jim's ever had," ultimately leads Huck to change his mind and to once again help Jim escape.

The incident leaves Huck viewing himself as a low and immoral person who may as well stop trying to be good. Huck is experiencing a conflict between the external forces of the society around him and internal force of his bond with Jim. For the reader, this is another example of dramatic irony, as we can clearly see that Huck's action, in preventing a fellow human being's permanent enslavement and separation from his family, is actually the moral decision, counteracting the actions of an immoral, though supposedly civilized, society.

Activity—Origins of Huck's Morality

The chapter is an important one to focus on with students, as it sets up the novel's eventual climax in chapter 31. The following steps, which can be completed individually or in pairs/groups, will prepare students for an engaging discussion on the events of the chapter:

Reread chapter 16.

Find at least three quotations that show Huck's struggle with his morality (or conscience) in this chapter.

Write at least one page answering the following questions:

- Where does Huck's morality, or sense of right and wrong, come from?
- Did he learn it, or is it just part of him?
- If it is learned, from where did he learn it?
- How is his morality changing?
- How is his struggle with his conscience ironic?

Discussions in history class will illuminate the potential gravity of Huck's actions in this chapter. Huck would have been considered by his society a *race traitor*, or one who takes sides with a black man over a white property owner. Just a few years later, Huck would have faced criminal prosecution under the Fugitive Slave Act of 1850.

The following activity will allow for further connections to history, and will make clear to students the precarious situation that Jim has gotten himself into.

Activity—Mapping Jim's Route to Freedom

In chapter 16, Jim and Huck are in search of Cairo, Illinois, eventually missing it in the fog. Distribute to students a blank map of the southern states, and project a copy of the same. Outline, or have them help you outline, the Mississippi River.

Next, identify some key locations for them, or have them find these locations with a partner or group: first, the starting point—Huck and Jim's hometown, which in the novel is identified as St. Joseph, Missouri. St. Joseph is fictional, but is generally agreed to be modeled after Twain's home of Hannibal, Missouri. Then, mark the locations of both Cairo and New Orleans, Louisiana.

It will also be useful to mark each of the surrounding states as either "free" or "slave" states. This can be done in history class, or in English class using information students learned in history.

Jim has escaped slavery along the Missouri-Illinois border, his owner having threatened to sell him down to New Orleans, at the bottom of the map. He is headed down the Mississippi River, in search of Cairo. Ask students: "Why Cairo?" Students may have a variety of suppositions, or may be aware that Cairo is where the Mississippi River meets the Ohio River, which can now also be traced on the map.

The map will provide students a visual, allowing them to see that if Jim can reach the Ohio River, it will take him north into "free" territory.

However, students will also be able to see that Jim initially escaped right on the border of Missouri (a slave state) and Illinois (a free state), so why couldn't he just cross into Illinois and be free?

Students will also be able to see, from the map, the significance of Huck and Jim having missed Cairo in the fog. They are now surrounded by slave states and are moving further south, a fact that will engage students in finding out what will happen next.

By discussing this map in both English and history class, students should come away from this activity understanding the following:

- Jim initially escaped after overhearing Miss Watson's intention to sell him down to New Orleans, which most certainly would have meant being sold at auction into the brutal plantation system.
- Escaping into Illinois, though a free state, would not have been enough. To truly escape, Jim would need to move far into the "free" northern states, which is why he sought the Ohio River.
- By missing the Ohio and now descending further south into slavery territory, Jim's situation is dangerous and hopeless.

This initial map activity will set the groundwork for the larger-scale mapping of Huck and Jim's journey that is described in the following section.

HUCK AND LINCOLN MAP PROJECT

As the class approaches the novel's climax in chapter 31, students will participate in a larger-scale map project that will serve as a study guide for their final assessment.

First of all, in either their English or history class, students will reproduce a large map of the Mississippi River (from Missouri down) on butcher paper, adding to the map key locations such as St. Joseph, the Phelps farm, and the homes of the Grangerford and Wilkes families. There are several resources online that can help students find these locations.

Students will then be placed into groups, and each group will be given a different extract from the novel. The extracts are from chapters 8 to 27. Each group will answer the following questions:

- What is happening in this scene?
- Explain the significance. What does this show us about Huck's views on race/slavery/Jim, and so on?

- What part should we cut out to put on the big map (this could be a sentence, a paragraph, etc.)? Hint: Look for the moment when we see a "shift" in Huck's thinking.
- Where should this go on the map? In other words, where does the scene take place, geographically? How do you know?

Each group, in a chosen location, will add to the map a "short" version of their extract (the portion that best exemplifies the significance of the passage), and a handwritten paragraph (this could be done on a half sheet of binder paper) explaining that significance.

The following are the six extracts to be used in this activity:

Chapter 8

> *"How do you come to be here, Jim, and how'd you get here?"*
>
> *He looked pretty uneasy, and didn't say nothing for a minute. Then he says:*
>
> *"Maybe I better not tell."*
>
> *"Why, Jim?"*
>
> *"Well, dey's reasons. But you wouldn' tell on me ef I uz to tell you, would you, Huck?"*
>
> *"Blamed if I would, Jim."*
>
> *"Well, I b'lieve you, Huck. I—I run off."*
>
> *"Jim!"*
>
> *"But mind, you said you wouldn' tell—you know you said you wouldn' tell, Huck."*
>
> *"Well, I did. I said I wouldn't, and I'll stick to it. Honest injun, I will. People would call me a low-down Abolitionist and despise me for keeping mum—but that don't make no difference. I ain't a-going to tell, and I ain't a-going back there, anyways. So, now, le's know all about it."*

Chapter 11

> *Then I jumped in the canoe and dug out for our place, a mile and a half below, as hard as I could go. I landed, and slopped through the timber and up the ridge and into the cavern. There Jim laid, sound asleep on the ground. I roused him out and says:*
>
> *"Git up and hump yourself, Jim! There ain't a minute to lose. They're after us!"*
>
> *Jim never asked no questions, he never said a word; but the way he worked for the next half an hour showed about how he was scared. By that time everything we had in the world was on our raft, and she was ready to be shoved out from the willow cove where she was hid. We put out the camp fire at the cavern the first thing, and didn't show a candle outside after that.*

Chapter 15

Jim looked at the trash, and then looked at me, and back at the trash again. He had got the dream fixed so strong in his head that he couldn't seem to shake it loose and get the facts back into its place again right away. But when he did get the thing straightened around he looked at me steady without ever smiling, and says:

"What do dey stan' for? I'se gwyne to tell you. When I got all wore out wid work, en wid de callin' for you, en went to sleep, my heart wuz mos' broke bekase you wuz los', en I didn' k'yer no' mo' what become er me en de raf'. En when I wake up en fine you back agin, all safe en soun', de tears come, en I could a got down on my knees en kiss yo' foot, I's so thankful. En all you wuz thinkin' 'bout wuz how you could make a fool uv ole Jim wid a lie. Dat truck dah is trash; en trash is what people is dat puts dirt on de head er dey fren's en makes 'em ashamed."

Then he got up slow and walked to the wigwam, and went in there without saying anything but that. But that was enough. It made me feel so mean I could almost kissed his foot to get him to take it back.

It was fifteen minutes before I could work myself up to go and humble myself to a nigger; but I done it, and I warn't ever sorry for it afterwards, neither. I didn't do him no more mean tricks, and I wouldn't done that one if I'd a knowed it would make him feel that way.

Chapter 16

"Good-bye, sir," says I; "I won't let no runaway niggers get by me if I can help it."

They went off and I got aboard the raft, feeling bad and low, because I knowed very well I had done wrong, and I see it warn't no use for me to try to learn to do right; a body that don't get started right when he's little ain't got no show—when the pinch comes there ain't nothing to back him up and keep him to his work, and so he gets beat. Then I thought a minute, and says to myself, hold on; s'pose you'd a done right and give Jim up, would you felt better than what you do now? No, says I, I'd feel bad—I'd feel just the same way I do now. Well, then, says I, what's the use you learning to do right when it's troublesome to do right and ain't no trouble to do wrong, and the wages is just the same? I was stuck. I couldn't answer that. So I reckoned I wouldn't bother no more about it, but after this always do whichever come handiest at the time.

Chapter 23

I went to sleep, and Jim didn't call me when it was my turn. He often done that. When I waked up just at daybreak he was sitting there with his head down betwixt his knees, moaning and mourning to himself. I didn't take notice nor let on. I knowed what it was about. He was thinking about his wife and his children, away up yonder, and he was low and homesick; because he hadn't ever been away from home before in his life; and I do believe he cared just as much for his people as white folks does for their'n. It don't seem natural, but I reckon it's so. He was often moaning and mourning that way nights, when he judged I was asleep, and saying, "Po' little 'Lizabeth! po' little Johnny! it's mighty hard; I spec' I ain't ever gwyne to see you no mo', no mo'!" He was a mighty good nigger, Jim was.

Chapter 27

So the next day after the funeral, along about noon-time, the girls' joy got the first jolt. A couple of nigger traders come along, and the king sold them the niggers reasonable, for three-day drafts as they called it, and away they went, the two sons up the river to Memphis, and their mother down the river to Orleans. I thought them poor girls and them niggers would break their hearts for grief; they cried around each other, and took on so it most made me down sick to see it. The girls said they hadn't ever dreamed of seeing the family separated or sold away from the town. I can't ever get it out of my memory, the sight of them poor miserable girls and niggers hanging around each other's necks and crying; and I reckon I couldn't a stood it all, but would a had to bust out and tell on our gang if I hadn't knowed the sale warn't no account and the niggers would be back home in a week or two.

The Climax of Huck's Evolution: Chapter 31

The final extract from the novel to be added to the map will come from chapter 31, in which Huck reaches the climax of his struggle. While reading the chapter, students should answer the following questions:

1. Describe in detail the struggle Huck has with his conscience in this chapter.
2. Which makes this struggle more difficult for Huck: external forces (such as society) or internal forces (within himself)? Explain.
3. How does Huck's struggle in this chapter demonstrate irony (particularly dramatic irony)?
4. The irony in this chapter creates satire. To what actions or beliefs of society is the satire pointed?
5. How does the irony and satire in this chapter help us to understand Mark Twain's *purpose* (what he is trying to show us)?

Students will then undergo the same process they did when placing the first six extracts on the map. The chapter 31 extract, however, will be chosen and discussed by the whole class.

Guide students in choosing a short extract from the chapter that best illustrates Huck's moral dilemma and his ultimate decision, and facilitate a discussion of the significance of the extract and of the scene in general.

A likely extract is the following:

> *I felt good and all washed clean of sin for the first time I had ever felt so in my life, and I knowed I could pray now. But I didn't do it straight off, but laid the paper down and set there thinking—thinking how good it was all this happened so, and how near I come to being lost and going to hell. And went on thinking. And got to thinking over our trip down the river; and I see Jim before me all the time: in the day and in the night-time, sometimes moonlight, sometimes storms, and we a-floating along, talking and singing and laughing. But somehow I couldn't seem to strike no places to harden me against him, but only the other kind. I'd see him standing my watch on top of his'n, 'stead of calling me, so I could go on sleeping; and see him how glad he was when I come back out of the fog; and when I come to him again in the swamp, up there where the feud was; and such-like times; and would always call me honey, and pet me and do everything he could think of for me, and how good he always was; and at last I struck the time I saved him by telling the men we had small-pox aboard, and he was so grateful, and said I was the best friend old Jim ever had in the world, and the only one he's got now; and then I happened to look around and see that paper.*
>
> *It was a close place. I took it up, and held it in my hand. I was a-trembling, because I'd got to decide, forever, betwixt two things, and I knowed it. I studied a minute, sort of holding my breath, and then says to myself:*
>
> *"All right, then, I'll go to hell"—and tore it up.*

The result of this map project will be a visual representation of Huck's morality evolving, particularly when it comes to questions of race. The next step is to connect this to Lincoln.

Juxtaposing Lincoln's Evolution with Huck's

The following extracts from Lincoln's letters and speeches demonstrate a similar evolution on the part of the sixteenth president. Students will discuss these documents and this evolution in their history class, eventually adding extracts from these documents to the large map, side by side with Huck's extracts.

Letter to Horace Greeley (1862)

> *If there be those who would not save the Union unless they could at the same time save Slavery, I do not agree with them. If there be those who would not save the Union unless they could at the same time destroy Slavery, I do not agree*

with them. My paramount object in this struggle is to save the Union, and is not either to save or destroy Slavery. If I could save the Union without freeing any slave, I would do it, and if I could save it by freeing all the slaves, I would do it, and if I could save it by freeing some and leaving others alone, I would also do that. What I do about Slavery and the colored race, I do because I believe it helps to save this Union and what I forbear, I forbear because I do not believe it would help to save the Union.

The Emancipation Proclamation (1862)

That on the first day of January, in the year of our Lord one thousand eight hundred and sixty-three, all persons held as slaves within any State or designated part of a State, the people whereof shall then be in rebellion against the United States, shall be then, thenceforward, and forever free; and the Executive Government of the United States, including the military and naval authority thereof, will recognize and maintain the freedom of such persons, and will do no act or acts to repress such persons, or any of them, in any efforts they may make for their actual freedom.

The Gettysburg Address (1863)

Four score and seven years ago our fathers brought forth on this continent, a new nation, conceived in Liberty, and dedicated to the proposition that all men are created equal.

Now we are engaged in a great civil war, testing whether that nation, or any nation so conceived and so dedicated, can long endure. We are met on a great battle-field of that war. We have come to dedicate a portion of that field, as a final resting place for those who here gave their lives that that nation might live. It is altogether fitting and proper that we should do this.

But, in a larger sense, we can not dedicate—we can not consecrate—we can not hallow this ground. The brave men, living and dead, who struggled here, have consecrated it, far above our poor power to add or detract. The world will little note, nor long remember what we say here, but it can never forget what they did here. It is for us the living, rather, to be dedicated here to the unfinished work which they who fought here have thus far so nobly advanced. It is rather for us to be here dedicated to the great task remaining before us—that from these honored dead we take increased devotion to that cause for which they gave the last full measure of devotion—that we here highly resolve that these dead shall not have died in vain—that this nation, under God, shall have a new birth of freedom—and that government of the people, by the people, for the people, shall not perish from the earth.

Second Inaugural Address (1865)

If we shall suppose that American slavery is one of those offenses which, in the providence of God, must needs come, but which, having continued through

His appointed time, He now wills to remove, and that He gives to both North and South this terrible war as the woe due to those by whom the offense came, shall we discern therein any departure from those divine attributes which the believers in a living God always ascribe to Him? Fondly do we hope, fervently do we pray, that this mighty scourge of war may speedily pass away. Yet, if God wills that it continue until all the wealth piled by the bondsman's two hundred and fifty years of unrequited toil shall be sunk, and until every drop of blood drawn with the lash shall be paid by another drawn with the sword, as was said three thousand years ago, so still it must be said "the judgments of the Lord are true and righteous altogether."

Students should understand that in 1862, as evidenced in his letter to Horace Greeley, Lincoln was ambivalent about ending slavery, seeing it as a means to an end—his purpose was to do whatever was most likely to preserve the Union—so that the Emancipation Proclamation was more of a political act and a strategic act than a moral act.

The following year, however, in the "Gettysburg Address," Lincoln acknowledges the need to reconcile as a nation, thereby implying—though not outright endorsing—the need to end slavery. The "Second Inaugural Address" demonstrates further evolution, as Lincoln clearly recognizes slavery as the great sin of our nation, and in the same year Lincoln supports passage of the 13th Amendment, ending slavery.

FINAL ASSESSMENT

The following is an example of the final assessment of an eighth-grade cross-curricular unit focused on Lincoln and Huck Finn. The exam addresses the following standards:

✍ Reading Standards for Literature

8RL1. Cite the textual evidence that most strongly supports an analysis of what the text says explicitly as well as inferences drawn from the text.

8RL2. Determine a theme or central idea of a text and analyze its development over the course of the text, including its relationship to the characters, setting, and plot; provide an objective summary of the text.

✍ Reading Standards for Literacy in History/Social Studies

6–8RH1. Cite specific textual evidence to support analysis of primary and secondary sources.

6–8RH6. Identify aspects of a text that reveal an author's point of view or purpose (e.g., loaded language, inclusion or avoidance of particular facts).

Instructions: Respond in paragraph form to each of the following questions. Include specific support from the relevant source material.

1. Compare and contrast Lincoln's position regarding emancipation in early 1862 with Huck's attitude toward helping Jim escape slavery in the first half of the novel. How did similar issues "divide" their loyalties? Use Lincoln's letter to Horace Greeley, the Emancipation Proclamation, and *The Adventures of Huckleberry Finn* (chapter 16, in particular) for support.
2. Using Lincoln's Second Inaugural Address and chapter 31 for support, discuss the extent to which both Lincoln's and Huck's positions evolved. Be sure to also discuss reasons for this evolution, using additional sources to illustrate those reasons.

The following are sample responses from an eighth-grade student:

1. *According to Lincoln's letter to Horace Greeley, Lincoln's "paramount object in this struggle is to save" the Union, and if that means making a decision—supporting it, abolishing it, a little bit of both—then so be it. Huck has a related issue because, at first, his main goal is to save himself; throughout the novel, he continuously considers leaving Jim in the night or saying he is going somewhere and not coming back. However, if helping Jim means freedom for Huck, he will do it.*

   Chapter 16 shows the readers Huck's internal conflict about his opinion of slavery and Jim. This is the scene where he finally begins to imagine life without Jim and how Jim would feel, too. Huck questions morality in the lines, "suppose you'd a done right and give Jim up" by looking through Jim's perspective and considering the effects. What really makes it right—wouldn't vaguely killing Jim be wrong, too? This is significant because it is the first time Huck truly thinks about his actions.
2. *While both Huck and Lincoln's main objectives are to save themselves—in Lincoln's case, his people of the Union—Huck gradually falls away from that without much consideration until near the end. Lincoln's goal is clear and permanent, but at the end of his letter to Horace Greeley, he mentions that his opinion of slavery may be altered. Within the next three years until his death, Lincoln comes to actively end slavery.*

   Huck is also growing, suddenly saving Jim, and by Chapter 31 he knows like he knows the patterns on his shirt that he "got to decide, forever, betwixt two things." Lincoln, likewise, as President, is very aware of this need, as President. In the end, stopping slavery is an important goal for both Huck and Lincoln, and they both risk their own lives for it.

SUMMARY

This chapter has provided strategies for helping students to appreciate the use of satire in a novel, and has demonstrated how to create an authentic cross-curricular unit of study that demands depth of knowledge of both literature and history. It is an example of how the two disciplines can work together to create rigorous learning experiences without compromising the use of literature in the classroom.

Here, again, a unit of study is incorporating nonfiction texts in the form of primary and secondary historical documents, thereby providing practice for students to work with nonfiction, yet the literature is still at the forefront of the unit, once again proving that the incorporation of nonfiction texts need not and should not *replace* the study of literature.

By devoting ample time to work with a partnering teacher, and devising both lessons and assessments that will have high stakes in two different classrooms, students have the opportunity to appreciate the real-life interconnectedness between disciplines and the importance of studying related material in tandem.

Index

The Adventures of Huckleberry Finn, 156–77
The Adventures of Huckleberry Finn: Robotic Edition, 159
The Adventures of Tom Sawyer, 161
allusion, 36, 47, 58, 61, 67, 76, 78
ambiguity, 41, 47, 57–58, 66, 71–72, 89, 98–99, 119, 122, 123, 139
"Ambush", 122–24
annotating text, 19, *22*, 23, *24*, 25, *26*, 27, 32, 34, 38, 40, 76, *77*, 78, 81, 82, 86, 89, 133, 135, 147, *148*
antagonist, 20, 49, 61, 94, 96, 100, 133

banned books, 157–58
Beloved, 140–47, *148*, 149–51, *152*, 153–55
Beowulf, 51
bildungsroman, 154
Bloom, Harold, 86
Bloom's Taxonomy, 114
Branagh, Kenneth, 71
The Brief Wondrous Life of Oscar Wao, 91
Burton, Richard, 71

The Canterbury Tales, 51
characterization, 22, 39, 41–43, 71–72, 75, 78–79, 85, 89, 93; static character, 71;dynamic character, 71; character foil, 88
circumlocution, 140, 142–44, 147, 154
climax, 59, 94, 96–101, 103, 111, 118–19, 129, 145, 161, 165, 166, 168, 171. *See also* exposition, plot, resolution, rising action
close reading, 14–28, 29, 34–46, 70, 74–75, 76–81, 86, 89, 93, 121, 135, 140, 143, 147, 151, 160–64
Common Core assessments, 5, 14, 46, 87–89, 136, 150, 155
Common Core College and Career Readiness Anchor Standards for 6th to 12th Grade Reading: R1, 15, 33, 48, 58, 60, 63, 69, 86, 116, 127, 156, 174; 8RL1, 174; 11-12RL1, 58; R2, 29, 48, 54, 60, 63, 69, 116, 126, 127, 140, 157, 174; 8RL2, 174; R3, 48, 60, 63, 69, 90, 141, 157; 9-10RL3, 69; R4, 15, 29, 69, 86, 116; 11-12RL4, 69, 116; R5, 48, 69, 91, 116, 127, 157; 8RL5, 157; 11-12RL5, 116, 157; R6, 30, 69, 116, 127, 141, 157; 8RL6, 160; 11-12RL6, 160; R7, 48, 56; 8RL7, 48, 56, 70; 11-12RL7, 48, 56, 70; R8, 30; R9, 30, 48, 70, 116, 141, 157; 9-10RL9, 48, 58–59, 70;

11–12RL9, 116, 157; R10, 30, 48, 70, 91, 116, 157
Common Core College and Career Readiness Anchor Standards for 6th to 12th Grade Speaking and Listening: SL1, 80, 83, 128, 137, 153; SL2, 80; SL3, 85; SL4, 40, 81, 85, 128, 137; SL5, 32, 83, 137; SL6, 83
Common Core College and Career Readiness Anchor Standards for 6th to 12th Grade Writing: W1, 1, 19, 37, 63, 84, 87, 135–136, 146, 153; W2, 1, 43, 84; W3, 91, *92*, 113; 8W3, *92;* 9-10W3, *92;* 11-12W3, *92;* W4, 1, 37, 151; W5, 1, 45, 84, 91, 111, 153; W7, 33; W8, 63, 149; W9, 43, 82, 86, 87, 135–136, 149; W10, 44, 82
Common Core Reading Standards for Literacy in History/Social Studies: 6-8RH1, 174; 6-8RH6, 175
concrete details, 20, 34, 42, 45, 101–102
conflict, 20, 49, 59, 61, 71, 72, 74, 76, 80, 90, 93, 94–101, 113, 118, 132, 166, 175; external conflict, 71, 95–97, 166; internal conflict, 71, 95–96, 166, 175. *See also* antagonist, climax, plot, protagonist, resolution, rising action
connotation, 17, 27, 36, 38, 39, 50, 78, 129, 135, 144, 147, 163. *See also* diction
Costa, Maddy, 64, 65
cross-curricular, 29, 31, 142, 149–51, 156. *See also* nonfiction, research

Death of a Salesman, ix
Diani and Devine, 159
Díaz, Junot, 91, 107
diction, 16–17, 19, 21, 25, 27, 36, 38–40, 71, 78–79, 109, 131–33, 143, 147. *See also* connotation
Douglass, Frederick, 150
"Dream Obits for Liz", 120
Dred Scott decision, 150, 164
Drown, 91

The Emancipation Proclamation, 173, 175
English language learners, xi, 16
essay writing: body paragraph, 5, 8; conclusion, 5, 9, 11; five-paragraph essay, 6; grading practices, 3, 5, 11, 84, 153–54; introduction, 7; peer review, 6, 111; revision, 5; textual evidence, 8–9, 19, 22, 43–44, 56, 61–62, 67, 73, 80, 85, 87, 89, 138, 153–54, 175; thesis, 5, 7–9, 11, 32, 155; titles, 7; topic sentence, 8. *See also* fiction writing, timed writing
evaluating an author's choices, x, 14, 16, 19, 22, 25, 27, 28, 37, 41, 54, 57, 90, 93, 101, 109, 118, 119, 120, 123, 124, 127, 133, 138
evaluating sources, 30–31, 33, 41, 138
existentialism, 72
exposition, 59, 61, 75, 79, 94–96, 100. *See also* climax, plot, resolution, rising action

"The Fall of the House of Usher", 15
The Fault in Our Stars, 158. *See also* banned books
fiction writing, 90–114; dialogue, 102–7; punctuation dialogue, 103–5, 113–14; narrative voice, 109–11. *See also* voice; pacing, 102–9, 113, 135; revision, 111; scene, 102, 111, 114; submitting student fiction, 113; summary, 102, 111. *See also* essay writing
"Fiesta 1980", 91, 96–99, 107, 109
figurative language, 109, 121. *See also* imagery
Finding Nemo, 95
Fitzgerald, F. Scott, 4, 29, 34, 36–37, 39, 41, 45
flashback, 97, 107–9, 130, 136, 145

foreshadowing, 16, 42, 58, 61, 70, 80, 118, 151
Freudian reading, 88
Frozen, 124
Fugitive Slave Act of 1850, 150, 167

Garner, Margaret, 150
gender expectations, 50, 53, 55, 61
The Gettysburg Address, 173
"Good Form", 122–24
Gotham Writer's Workshop, 99
The Grapes of Wrath, 19, 143
The Great Gatsby, 3, 29–46
Greeley, Horace, 172, 175
ground situation, 49, 94–96, 98, 100. *See also* conflict, exposition, inciting incident

hamartia, 34
Hamlet, 51, 53, 68–76, *77*, 78–89, 141
Hawke, Ethan, 71
Hawthorne, Nathaniel, 141
Hemingway, Ernest, 106
Henry IV, 53, 60
"Hills Like White Elephants", 106
"How to Talk to Your Mother (Notes)", 120
"How to Tell a True War Story", 121–22
hyperbole, 76

imagery, 16, 18, 19, 21, 36–40, 80, 85, 130–131, 133, 135, 144–45, 147, 154
inciting incident, 49, 94–96, 100, 103
inference, 17, 19, 21, 25, 55, 62, 80, 93, 143, 146
in media res, 107
intercalary chapters, 143, 147
International Baccalaureate (IB), ix, 2
"In the Field", 124–27
irony, 159, 160–64, 167, 171; dramatic irony, 159–60, 162, 164, 166, 171; situational irony, 159; verbal irony, 159–61
iTunes U, ix

The Jazz Age, 33, 37, 43
juxtaposition, 129, 131, 134

The Kite Runner, 141

Lee, Harper, 19, 158
Lincoln, Abraham, 156, 164–66, 168, 172–77; letter to Horace Greeley (1862), 172, 175; second inaugural address (1865), 173–75
lost generation, 34, 37, 43, 45
"Love", 120–21

Macbeth, ix, 9
magical realism, 140, 142, 147–49
"The Man I Killed", 122–24
The Merry Wives of Windsor, 60
metafiction, 115, 117, 120, 124, 127–28, 130–31, 134, 136–37
Metamorphoses, 58
metaphor, 16, 85, 87, 145
A Midsummer Night's Dream, 53
MLA formatting, 33, 138
modernism, 29, 34, 118–19
Monson, Ander, 120
mood, 16–19, 21, 22, 25, 27, 72, 74, 76, 151
Moore, Lorrie, 93, 120
Morrison, Toni, 140, 142, 143–44, 146–47, 149–51, 154
motif, 36, 38, 40, 43, 53, 58, 70–71, 74, 78–79, 81, 85, 88, 93, 124–125, 129, 134, 136–37, 144–45

narrative distance, 120, 127
New South Books, 158
nonfiction, xi, xii, 31, 32, 42, 45, 117, 121–25, 127, 142, 150–51, 155, 176
"Notes", 124–27

O'Brien, Tim, 115, 117
oedipal complex, 88
Oedipus Rex, 141
Of Mice and Men, 97

One Flew over the Cuckoo's Nest, 141
Ovid, 58

paradox, 72, 122, 123, 145. *See also* ambiguity
plot, 39, 49, 59, 70, 94–101, 113, 117, 132, 164. *See also* climax, conflict, exposition, ground situation, inciting incident, resolution, rising action
Poe, Edgar Allan, 15
point of view, 41–42, 44, 101, 120, 123, 126–27, 144, 161
postmodernism, 115–39, 142
pre-reading, 30–34, 49–52, 73–74, 157–60
protagonist, 20, 49, 61, 75, 94–101, 111. *See also* antagonist, characterization, conflict

Queen, 73

realism, 119
repetition, 25, 36, 109, 123–24, 127, 133
research, 30–34, 42, 45, 138, 149–51, 155. *See also* cross-curricular, evaluating sources, nonfiction
resolution, 59, 70, 90, 94, 97–101, 111, 118, 129, 138. *See also* climax, exposition, plot, rising action
rising action, 59, 94, 96–98, 100–101, 103, 111, 118, 129. *See also* climax, exposition, plot, resolution
roaring twenties, 34, 37
romanticism, 119

satire, 158–60, 163–64, 171, 176
Saunders, George, 19, 93
setting, 49, 59, 61
Shakespearean conventions, 58; allusions, 58, 76; aside, 75; bawdy humor, 47, 59, 60, 62; comic characters, 47, 59; comic relief, 59, 88; five act structure, 47, 59, 88; monologue, 72; play within a play, 53–54, 61, 88; pun, 59, 60, 72; role reversal, 59–61, 63, 65–67; soliloquy, 72, 75–76, 78–80, 85, 88; strong women, 9, 47, 60
Shakespearean language, 50–52, 70–71; contractions, 51–52; pronouns, 52; syntax, 52
Shakespeare, William, viii, 9, 47–89, 141
showing, not telling, 20, 101–2, 113, 114
Slaughterhouse Five, ix, 115, 117, 128–39
Socratic seminar, 73, 81, 85, 140, 153
"so what?", 11–14, 22, 25, 28, 36, 40, 80, 118, 134, 151. *See also* close reading, evaluating an author's choices
"Speaking of Courage", 124–27
Steinbeck, John, 19, 97, 143
"Sticks", 19, 22, *23, 24*
style, ix, 9, 93, 109, 115, 133, 135, 142, 144–45
subtext, 105–7, 114
The Sun Also Rises, ix
surrealism, 131, 133–34, 137, 139–40, 142
symbolism, 16, 34, 36, 42–43, 45, 72, 134, 143–45, 151, 165

The Taming of the Shrew, 47–67
The Taming of the Shrew (1967 film), 57, 64–66
The Taming of the Shrew (1980 BBC film) 57, 64
"The Taming of the Shrew: This is Not a Woman Being Crushed", 64, 65
Taney, Roger B. (Chief Justice of U.S. Supreme Court), 164
TED Talks, 31
theme, 16, 39, 43, 47, 53, 56, 58, 61, 72, 74, 79–81, 85, 89, 93, 96, 125–26, 134, 137, 140, 142–43, 145–47, 154–55

The Things They Carried, ix, 115–28
"The Things They Carried", 117, 120, 123, 125
timed writing, 4, 6, 9–11, 37, 45, 63, 81–82, 87, 136–37
To Kill a Mockingbird, 19, 158
tone, 22, 38–39, 154
Twain, Mark, 141, 156, 158, 161, 164, 167, 171

underground railroad, 150
"Under Pressure", 73
unreliable narrator, 41, 120, 127, 161

voice, 109–11, 115, 130–35, 139, 142–43, 150, 154, 161. *See also* fiction writing
Vonnegut, Kurt, 115, 128–31, 133–35, 137

Wall-E, 95
What If? Writing Exercises for Fiction Writers, 99
Whitman, Walt, 141
Wolff, Tobias, 93

Zeffirelli, Franco, 57, 62, 65–66

About the Authors

Elizabeth James graduated from the University of California, Davis, in 2006 with a bachelor's degree in English. She began teaching English at a Title I school in Stockton, California, in 2007. She has spent the last four years as the International Baccalaureate coordinator at her site. She and Bill share two loud, sticky, wonderful boys together: Tom and Sam. This is her first book.

B. H. James's novel, *Parnucklian for Chocolate*, was a finalist for the 2014 PEN Center USA Literary Award in Fiction. His short fiction, creative non-fiction, and drama have appeared in various online and print journals. James received his MFA in fiction from the University of Nebraska, Omaha, in 2010. He has taught high school English in Stockton, California, for the past nine years.